T0339835

Mediating
History

This book has been funded by NATIONAL VIDEO RESOURCES,

a project of THE ROCKEFELLER FOUNDATION.

Consulting Editor: Louise Spain

Mediating History

THE MAP GUIDE TO INDEPENDENT VIDEO

by and about

AFRICAN AMERICAN, ASIAN AMERICAN,

LATINO, AND NATIVE AMERICAN PEOPLE

Edited by

Barbara Abrash and Catherine Egan

The Media Alternatives Project
Avery Fisher Center for Music and Media
Bobst Library
New York University

NEW YORK UNIVERSITY PRESS
New York and London

Copyright © 1992 by New York University
All rights reserved
Manufactured in the United States of America

Library of Congress Cataloging-in-Publication Data
Mediating history: the MAP guide to independent video by and about African American, Asian
   American, Latino, and Native American people
   edited by Barbara Abrash and Catherine Egan
         p. cm.
      ISBN 0-8147-0619-3 (cl.) -- ISBN 0-8147-0620-7 (pbk.)
      1. Minorities--United States--Video catalogs.
      2. Minorities in motion pictures.

   I. Abrash, Barbara.
   II. Egan, Catherine.
   E184.A1M36   1992
   016.79143 620693--dc20   92-22251
                        CIP

New York University Press books are printed on acid-free paper,
and their binding materials are chosen for strength and durability.

Book design Sandy Kaufman
Cover design Jennifer Lawson
Photo collage Frank Poueymirou
Book production Lorraine A. Williams

c 10 9 8 7 6 5 4 3 2 1
p 10 9 8 7 6 5 4 3 2 1

Contents

Acknowledgments

The Media Alternatives Project (MAP) is funded by National Video Resources, a program of The Rockefeller Foundation. Particular thanks go to Alberta Arthurs of The Rockefeller Foundation and to Gretchen Dykstra, former director of NVR, for their invaluable guidance and enthusiastic support. The editors also wish to thank Carlton C. Rochell, Dean of the New York University Libraries, whose commitment to video and emerging technologies led to the creation of the Avery Fisher Center for Music and Media which provides MAP with that all-important element, a home base.

MAP has benefited enormously from the contributions of a large and active group of advisors which includes scholars, teachers, writers, programmers, and film and video makers. Three of these advisors—Steve Brier, Louise Spain, and Janet Sternburg—deserve special mention for their efforts on MAP's behalf. We also extend sincere thanks and appreciation to the following: Claire Andrade-Watkins, Patricia Aufderheide, Deirdre Boyle, George Burdeau, Cheryl Chisholm, Christine Choy, Will Covington, Loni Ding, Linda Earle, Donald Fixico, Thelma Foote, Michael Frisch, Henry Louis Gates, Jr., Linda Gibson, Faye Ginsburg, William Greaves, Rayna Green, Mable Haddock, Lillian Jiménez, Elaine Kim, Dai Sil Kim-Gibson, Lisa Livingston, Beni Matias, Martha de Montana, Chon Noriega, Lucille Rhodes, Donald Rieck, Marlon Riggs, Robert Rosenstone, Vicki Ruiz, Emelia Seubert, Jacqueline Shearer, Beverly Singer, Robert Stam, George Stoney, Diosa Summers, Beverly Teach, Robert Toplin, Daniel Walkowitz, Elizabeth Weatherford, Lise Yasui, and Susan Zeig.

A number of our colleagues at Bobst Library have brought their unique backgrounds and expertise to this project. In particular, we wish to thank Angela Carreño, Lise Dyckman, Steven Higgins, Nancy Kranich, Leah Siegel, and Kent Underwood for their thoughtful contributions. Even closer to home, the Avery Fisher Center staff—especially Tony Cokes, Michael Gaffney, Veronica Paíz, and Donald Trammel—have given generously of their time and talents.

Special thanks go to those individuals who have worked with us at every stage in the preparation of this book. Consulting editor Louise Spain spent many hours listening, reviewing, and discussing issues of format. She provided consistently sound advice, especially in respect to the indexes. Assistant editor Kimberly Everett has been an essential member of the MAP team in every phase, from conceptualizing the project through production. Thanks also to Merritt Abrash for his critical eye and editorial advice.

The film and video annotations were written by Judith Trojan, Linda Gibson, Chon Noriega, Emelia Seubert, and MAP staff with the valuable assistance of Loni Ding and Linda Earle. Many distributors generously provided preview cassettes and detailed filmographic information.

Finally, our thanks to the staff of Bobst Library's Microcomputer Center for preparation of the camera-ready copy, and to NYU's Office of Advertising and Publications for the book design and layout.

Introduction

The Media Alternatives Project (MAP) was established in 1990 to introduce multicultural perspectives into American history teaching in colleges and universities through the use of independent film and video. Through its workshops, conferences, and publications, the Project seeks to introduce faculty, media selectors, and programmers to the value of these alternative media resources.

Despite the growing use of video in history classrooms, independently-produced works—which include many thought-provoking, intellectually exciting offerings—are among the least known and least accessible resources. And it is precisely these non-mainstream productions that most consistently challenge traditional perceptions, question conventional wisdom, and posit alternative ways of representing and interpreting history and culture.

Mediating History: The MAP Guide to Independent Video by and about African American, Asian American, Latino, and Native American People is an introduction to this work. The guide provides the following information:

- a selective annotated listing of 126 videotapes useful in teaching American history;
- contextualizing essays that identify important themes and issues, and ways of introducing independently-produced media into history teaching;
- a directory of alternative media information resources including journals, media arts organizations, and distributors;
- indices (title, subject, and chronological).

The book is organized in such a way that readers may go directly to what they need. Thus, the faculty member who has never used video in the classroom may wish to begin with Deirdre Boyle's essay "Critical Doubts and Differences: Independent Video and Teaching History," which speaks to concerns historians may have about the value of the visual media to a traditionally print-based discipline. While acknowledging commonly held prejudices and misconceptions about media—as well as some legitimate apprehension about scheduling and using unfamiliar equipment—Boyle argues persuasively for including independent video in the history curriculum.

But even history professors who are advocates for using media in instruction and who wish to introduce innovative, culturally diverse works may wonder how this is best accomplished. Because independently-produced videos tend to challenge the traditional categories and rules of academic history, and because they look and sound different from more conventional productions, they require thoughtful integration into the syllabus. In her essay "Multicultural Video in the Teaching of History," Patricia Aufderheide outlines ways this may be done and encourages faculty to experiment in presenting this material. For example, videos which include controversial ideas can, if they are properly introduced, lead students into uniquely productive classroom debates. Aufderheide also points out that videotapes need not be shown in their entirety—as with books, portions may be selected for screening and analysis. Aufderheide's approach serves to demystify the video medium and encourage faculty to make it work for them.

Media selectors and programmers will find Mediating History a useful collection development tool and thematic programming guide. The main body of the book has been organized into chapters dealing with African-American, Asian-American, Latino, and Native American content, respectively. (The Latino section is composed of Chicano and Puerto Rican work, reflecting the two communities most active in the production of media on social and historical subjects.) This grouping is not to suggest that these categories are homogeneous or parallel in their subjects and concerns, but rather recognizes the ways in which film and videomakers have identified themselves and their work at this time. A fifth category, "Crossing Boundaries," introduces work—either experimental in form or intercultural in subject matter—that points in future directions.

Each chapter consists of a brief essay addressing the principal themes contained in the videos, along with background notes about the social and political movements that gave rise to the work and comments about significant production techniques. The authors, each of whom is an authority on the work being discussed, also suggest effective ways of presenting it. Each essay is followed by a list of recommended titles, fully annotated with accompanying filmographic information. A short supplementary list of more briefly-noted titles suggests the range of work open for further exploration.

Finally, the "Alternative Media Resources" section provides information about distributors, organizations, festivals, and publications to assist media specialists and faculty in the tasks of locating and purchasing multicultural media.

The titles listed here were chosen by more than one hundred scholars, media selectors, and programmers who were asked to recommend independently-produced work on the basis of quality, creativity, relevance to teaching U.S. history, and presentation of new information and points of view. Although many of these titles have been seen on public television, our emphasis has been on film and video productions that grow out of personal commitment and social vision rather than the requirements of mass media. Many of these works were originally produced on film, but all of them are readily available for rental or purchase on videocassette.

Most are documentary in style, but some independently-produced dramatic films, such as THE BALLAD OF GREGORIO CORTEZ, are included for the importance of their presentation of historical information and fresh perspectives. Others, such as HISTORY AND MEMORY, push the boundaries of conventional documentary, suggesting new ways of representing history. Priority has been given to work made by members of the groups whose history and culture is being represented, but exceptions have been made in cases where partnerships have produced films and videos that place the perspectives of their subjects at the center. This is especially true of Native American work because until quite recently there have been few native producers. Several Canadian productions, such as FOSTER CHILD,

that deal with subjects significant to Native American life in the United States, have also been included.

We offer this guide as a work-in-progress, an invitation to join a continuing discussion about the role of the visual media, and multicultural video in particular, in the telling of American history. It is part of a much larger project of re-envisioning American history, a project which has found independent film and videomakers in the vanguard.

BARBARA ABRASH
CATHERINE EGAN

Multicultural Video in the Teaching of History

Patricia Aufderheide

T his guide to independently-made videos by and about African American, Asian American, Latino and Native American people introduces new voices into history teaching. It helps to bring alive the complex polycultural history you want your students to grasp. These videos give students visual images to anchor their learning. They also open up basic issues of history and historical research.

With this guide you can explore media resources which have been made by independent producers—people who make films and videos out of a passion for discovery and self-discovery. They address, sometimes by exploring their own identities and histories, issues that touch the history of the whole society. But while independent production has flourished in the last fifteen years, general knowledge about this work, and its distribution, has not developed as rapidly.

These videos are valuable to historians precisely because they offer a source of imagery often either erased or distorted in mainstream media. They do not present simply "another side" of the story; more significantly, they expose the fact that "the story" depends on the perspective of the teller. This is an opportunity for students to realize that history is a process that we actually live, not a set of dead facts.

Most of the videos listed here are documentary in nature, but those that are fiction are also valuable historical resources. Some deal with pre-twentieth century history. Many more deal with modern history and contemporary issues that command an explanation of their origins. All of them can provoke students to care about our culturally diverse American heritage.

History, often seen as a fixed text—and often told from the point of view of the "winners"—can be transformed into a process in which truth is always contested ground. History becomes, in this process, a battlefield for legitimacy; facts are ammunition in the stories we tell. These videos can invite discussion of the fact that American history is polycultural and that many different groups have struggled to realize this nation's democratic promise.

For instance, two films dealing with the military—THE MASSACHUSETTS 54TH COLORED INFANTRY and NISEI SOLDIER—offer concrete examples of where and how African American and Asian American people worked for equality and dignity. While revealing deep themes of discrimination in one of the nation's major institutions, they also reveal heroic, patriotic action by unsung people. Students might be stimulated to ask what these films say about the circumstances of daily life for different American groups in that period. What drove those men to volunteer for dangerous work, and at what cost to their families? What does their treatment say about social relationships at the time?

Students might also ask why an African-American or an Asian-American filmmaker bothered to dig into the past of soldiering. It is clearly not simple ethnic or gender identification. Loni Ding, for instance, is a Chinese-American woman who made a film about Japanese-American men. But both filmmakers are curious about communities and experiences that traditional texts often reduce to objects and references. How does their storytelling differ from other, more familiar texts on the Civil War and World War II? Who are their protagonists and major characters? What are their major events? What stereotypes of military history do their historical interpretations challenge?

Many of these videos go beyond the history of political events and leaders. When historians focus on the stories of men in positions of official power, they can't

help but imply that history is primarily made by such figures. Independent videomakers, while acknowledging the role and influence of such people, often provide another view of history and who makes it. And that gives back to the process of history its dynamism and complexity.

Some of the work described here shows how popular culture influences our perceptions of history and of each other. These videos demonstrate that cultural context shapes experience and possibility. ETHNIC NOTIONS, for instance, dramatically demonstrates the ways in which movies, cartoons, popular music, advertisements, and even lawn ornaments express and shape changing popular attitudes on racial issues. (This would be a good video to use in segments over the course of a survey class.) Those students who argue that pop culture shouldn't be weighted down with deep significance are confronted with evidence that makes them rethink how their ideas are affected by the images around them.

While ETHNIC NOTIONS shows how popular culture can denigrate, PLENA IS WORK, PLENA IS SONG shows how it can celebrate. It provides an historical and social context for Puerto Rican popular music; it shows that *plena*, like reggae, was fueled by economic and political conflict, and became a kind of oral newspaper of working people.

The profile of the Cuban jazz artist, MACHITO, introduces students to major artists whose influence on popular culture has been powerful. I REMEMBER HARLEM gives students a sense of the social context of cultural and political movements such as the Harlem Renaissance and the civil rights movement. LA OFRENDA traces the history of a popular festival from the streets of San Francisco back to pre-Columbian cultures.

With these videos, the history of major social movements can come to life, often told by participants or people invested in recovering those people's stories. They get to hear a version of the story that is clearly both personal and cultural. When students watch LA OPERACION, about forced sterilization in Puerto Rico, they learn about movements for Puerto Rican autonomy and women's rights from the perspective of those most intimately involved. They might ask why sterilization policies existed, and discover how they were justified.

With such videos, students are introduced to the concept of the "usable past"—we learn about the past to help make sense of the present. Productions such as THE LEMON GROVE INCIDENT, which dramatizes a showdown between a group of Mexican-American parents and their local school board over what the parents saw as *de facto* segregation in a California school, and "Eyes on the Prize," a documentary series about the civil rights movement, show how hard people have struggled—and have had to work, against the odds—to make basic democratic guarantees come true.

These two productions challenge many preconceptions. They turn people who had long been treated as objects of policy (and of history-telling) into subjects of their own drama (and of this history-telling). They put flesh and bones on familiar civics concepts, and make students realize that equality and dignity must be won. And they expose students to the fact that this history matters today.

These independent works can also help students understand that all history involves interpretation. For instance, MANOS A LA OBRA offers a harshly critical Puerto Rican perspective on Operation Bootstrap, which has often been celebrated as a successful economic development project. Students who are familiar with textbook descriptions of Operation Bootstrap may not be convinced by the argument presented in MANOS A LA OBRA, and after seeing the film might even be persuaded to have a classroom debate about it. As they take sides and assume historical roles, historical facts become their data for interpretation; they see historical narrative, such as the boldly point-of-view narration of MANOS A LA OBRA, as the argument it is; and history's importance to different groups also becomes evident. But even after debating the subject, some students might ask: What is the real story? The right story? What is the truth?

In the fiction feature THE BALLAD OF GREGORIO CORTEZ, these are central questions. The film concerns a legendary Mexican outlaw in turn-of-the-century Texas. On the basis of extensive historical research, the film tells and retells the story from the perspectives of the main characters (the "outlaw," his relatives, the Texas Rangers, a travelling journalist) and Anglo and Mexican bystanders, and also from the perspective of popular folk songs. Scenes are played and replayed in

flashback from the points of view of different characters. By the end, there are no villains left, only complex, tragic truths. THE BALLAD OF GREGORIO CORTEZ is, among other things, about the transformation of history into myth. And it is about the reality that there may be many truths in a situation.

After viewing, students might want to take on the role of a journalist whose job it is to tell the "real" story (each journalist identifying his or her audience, noting how that audience shapes the way the story is told). Or they might use the model of THE BALLAD OF GREGORIO CORTEZ to explore the historical construction of other larger-than-life figures. As they do so, they will be practicing some basic critical viewing skills. They will notice, for instance, how a camera angle or the framing of a shot, the pacing of a scene, the cueing of sound effects and music, all influence the conclusions they draw.

Several of these videos lay bare the adventure of doing historical research. FAMILY GATHERING chronicles the filmmaker's discovery of the long-buried history of Japanese-American internment in her own family. We watch as people deny and then grudgingly acknowledge this bitter period of their own pasts. The filmmaker has, by the end of the film, bridged the gap between private memory and public record.

Students could analyze the filmmaker's oral history methods (they can conduct such interviews themselves, with camcorders). They might ask themselves why the filmmaker's family so resisted remembering, and what our historical understanding of that period is like without their memories. Similarly, after watching IDA B. WELLS: A PASSION FOR JUSTICE, a biography of the crusading African-American journalist, students might make a list of the filmmaker's sources and discuss how they are used, which source has the most authority for them, and what other sources they might have wanted to use if they had made the film.

The recuperation of memory is also the recuperation of identity, against a dominant history that eliminates certain voices and experiences. HISTORY AND MEMORY, for instance, which traces a Japanese-American family's experience of internment camps through family mementos and official records, showcases the intersection of personal and public. Students might explore the implications—

both for a person and for the larger society—of the fact that private history is largely invisible in dominant narratives about the past.

For many Native Americans, however, private memory and shared history may converge. ITAM HAKIM, HOPIIT—featuring a Hopi who is among the last of his storytelling clan, essentially the historian of the tribe—reveals the way images and narratives of a collective past are shaped and communicated in one Native American tribe. Video work by Native Americans introduces students to different ways of understanding what history may be, as well as what kinds of research tools are appropriate to do it.

Videotapes that deal with recent rather than earlier periods may seem less like historical resources, but they can provide a topical anchor for historical trends. Take, for instance, WHO KILLED VINCENT CHIN?, about the murder by white autoworkers of a Chinese-American on whom they vented their rage at Japanese automobile industry competition. The tape offers frank discussion of enduring discrimination in American culture. It also illuminates historical issues such as the evolution of industrial culture and the tensions that emerged. Finally, in its comparison of nightly TV news reports and the stories told by the families involved, it demonstrates that sharply contrasting perspectives come not only from different ethnic groups but also from the kind of media used to tell the story. WHO KILLED VINCENT CHIN? gives students a current "hook" for issues that run through American history; you might even want to use it to begin a section (say, on immigration) and work backward.

Independent videos use a wide variety of sources to represent the past. Those sources include oral history, archival film, and family photographs. Videos may also use archival materials in very different ways, and students can see how such use shapes the story they are told. "Eyes on the Prize," for instance, is composed largely of compilation footage from contemporary news programs. Using stop-frame, search, and replay features on the videocassette recorder, students can review the process by which the filmmakers assembled their story, and closely look at the materials the filmmakers worked with. Why were cameras there? Who was holding the camera? Who did they focus on? How does the image differ or agree with the narration?

One advantage of this process is that, even if you do it only once in class, students suddenly perceive any filmed reality as a crafted product. They begin to see the process of creating history everywhere—including on the nightly news.

As you work with these videos, you will discover new ways to use them. It is not always necessary to show the whole tape; a small segment may be suitable to initiate discussion. You probably will give the students reading that brings in other perspectives. You also don't have to "cover all the ground." When students learn about the interpretation of one historical incident, they learn that interpretation is always a part of making history.

One thing that will make a big difference in your use of these materials is to share with students the background on the making of the videos—basic questions such as who made it, why, when, and with what audience in mind. When the students understand authorship, they can also claim their own right to critique it and to imagine how it might have been made differently.

This guide only scratches the surface of burgeoning video expression. As independent video production grows, along with your own creative use of it, you will find the sources listed here increasingly helpful in guiding you to new titles, distributors, and critical commentary.

Copyright ©1992 Patricia Aufderheide

Avery Fisher Center, Bobst Library

Critical Doubts and Differences

INDEPENDENT VIDEO AND TEACHING HISTORY

Deirdre Boyle

The greatest difficulty to overcome in introducing video into your history curriculum may be resolving your own doubts and fears about its use. Most educated Westerners have been taught to believe that language, especially the written word, is the only legitimate medium for serious, intellectual discourse. We have it on highest authority: "In the beginning was the Word." If you have ever been asked, "Did you teach today, or did you show a film?" you know the thinly-veiled contempt that question masks: you must be pandering to the lowest standards of scholarly inquiry and debate, caving in to pressures to entertain rather than inform, or simply taking the day off. Facing up to your colleagues' misconceptions and prejudices—and maybe your own—is the first step.

Next you will have to confront a host of practical problems. The bureaucratic logistics of dealing with video equipment and tapes in an institutional setting can stymie even the most enthusiastic. Once you have persuaded a department chair to budget for video, secured the cooperation of related support services in the university, previewed and selected the program, ordered the equipment, and prepared your students for new material, your program can still be sabotaged in a number of ways. There is nothing so humiliating as scheduling a tape for your class and then having to wing it when a disaster scenario plays itself out: the equipment is broken or fails to arrive; the wrong title is sent. Fortunately, videotapes are far more user-friendly than 16mm film ever was, and although video will require extra attention to detail and flexibility in dealing with snafus, the advantages far outweigh the risks entailed.

Video, as it is used throughout this volume, includes films on videotape as well as original video productions. There are several reasons why video rather than film is becoming the medium of choice at most academic institutions. Aside from the superiority of playback decks to film projectors in terms of costs, maintenance, and simplicity of operation, the ease with which a tape can be searched forward and backward to locate a specific scene and replay it is of particular value in classroom analysis. And tapes can usually be purchased or rented for less than comparable 16mm films.

Spurred by growing interest in cultural diversity and greater accessibility to media equipment and training, African Americans, Native Americans, Asian Americans, and Latinos have created a significant body of independent films and videotapes about their own histories. Their productions are relatively independent from commercial constraints, conventional styles, and traditional interpretations fostered by mainstream media and the dominant culture. It may take years to raise sufficient funding to produce an independent video, usually with little hope of ever seeing a profit on the actual investment of time, money, labor, and commitment required to make it. But there is the freedom to explore a subject with integrity, bound only by the limits of the filmmaker's determination, talent, and credit line.

The history revealed in these videos is interpreted by participant observers, not the so-called detached, objective observers who speak with the uniform voice of white male authority. Instead, one finds multiple voices inflected by the particular race, gender, and ethnicity of their subjects. Their stories, hitherto told by "others" if they have been told at all, are re-presented and re-interpreted from within a cultural perspective that restores authority to the cultural group, often revealing hidden, denied, and obscured aspects of the past. Intermixing interviews, archival footage, reenactments, omniscient narrators, and subjective viewpoints, these independent producers adapt familiar film formats to accommodate their more radical

aspirations, often creating hybrid forms to explore hybrid histories.

Some excellent feature-length fiction films have been made by independents—films such as TO SLEEP WITH ANGER and THE BALLAD OF GREGORIO CORTEZ. Although full-length films may seem too sprawling for in-class presentations, an entertaining fiction film can spark student interest in an historical period while simultaneously raising questions about the ways commercial films have shaped—and often misshaped—our vision of America's past. Given the limited time of most class periods, the more likely choice may be a half-hour or hour-long documentary. The deficiencies of some educational films—banal, predictable, and ideologically safe—contrast sharply with the freshness and challenges offered by independent documentaries made by polycultural producers. Although some students may write off documentary as dull, more will expect stimulating analysis and interpretation, influenced by recent successful public television series such as "The Civil War" and "Eyes on the Prize."

Given this wealth of independent productions on topics in American history, how should you use them in your curriculum? There is no one way to present a video. It is usually easy to leave a videocassette on reserve in a library, media center, or language lab, or loan it directly to a student to view: there are times when these may be the most efficient ways to treat screenings—as outside assignments. But there are compelling reasons for screening a video in class, making it central to your course. The experience of seeing a program with twenty other people and discovering through discussion that they have seen twenty different films is a powerful departure point for discussion about diversity, how different viewpoints and cultural identities affect interpretation of the same material. At times, subject matter may take a back seat to discussion of how the methods employed by the filmmaker influenced different interpretations among the group.

One does not need to be an expert about film to do this. Invariably I find my students, when given the chance, have far more to say about a tape than I had hoped for. By raising issues on their own, they gain confidence in their ability to analyze and interpret while discovering the potential for divergent views. It is always good for the teacher to be prepared by first previewing the video, jotting down the questions that might be raised when reading a written history: What kinds of sources are used? How is an event being illustrated or dramatized? Whose point of view is being presented? What authority is being established? Then there are basic questions about the relationship between form and content: How does the style influence the film's content and credibility? How does the use of sound (music, ambient noise, texts, and narrators) and image (photographs, archival footage, interviews, and reenactments) influence your emotional response to and intellectual grasp of the events and ideas presented?

When screening in class, some may prefer to lecture at length before the screening, saving any discussion for the next class session. Others may begin with a brief introduction, then screen the tape, and follow immediately with discussion. There are advantages to both approaches: providing space between screening and discussion can allow students to process their notes and responses, complete readings, and come prepared for discussion. Discussion following a screening allows you to get immediate impressions before students have had a chance to conform their ideas to what critics, scholars, or classmates have said about the work. You can then draw out complex or hidden associations in the tape, building on students' varied reactions and interpretations. Having used both methods, I prefer the spontaneity and dynamic quality of the latter approach. Discussion works best in smaller groups but can be successful with up to forty students. If your course is lecture-oriented and designed for a larger audience, discussion may seem like a luxury, but including some form of discussion will be especially valuable when using video.

I provide students with selected readings—reviews of the video, interviews with the director, essays about the subject matter and any issues raised by the methods used in the tape. (Distributors are often a good source of readings about their own video titles, occasionally providing you with copies of articles and reviews as well as citations.) These can be given out a week or more in advance, directly after the screening, or after the discussion. By varying these approaches, you will see the advantages of each and discover what works best with your students and your own teaching style.

Having students take detailed notes during screenings essentially alters their expectations about video. The effort involved in writing notes (whether verbal shorthand, cartoon storyboards, or some combination of both) focuses attention, heightens memory and recall, and encourages a more aware state of mind than is the norm for television viewing. Although students will complain they can't watch a tape *and* write about it, after a few sessions most will not only adjust to the discipline, they will appreciate it as they see the results of their critical viewing. I resist demands for a list of film terms or sample notes, encouraging students to invent their own language. The aim is for them to be able to read their notes and recreate the film in their mind's eye. I have them type one set of notes, which I read and return with comments, asking those who are floundering to submit notes for an additional video to check on progress. Students often ask to see the video first and take notes on a second viewing. If a tape is rented for a limited time period, repeated viewing may not be possible, but even if you own the tape, insist the first viewing include note-taking. Creating that shift in consciousness and attention is critical, and note-taking is the best way I know to jog the viewer out of the passivity induced by years of watching television.

If you allow for video as a legitimate medium for conducting and presenting historical research and analysis, if you hear the polyphony of America's voices and appreciate the different perspectives they convey, and if you create a safe space where students feel free to explore their own diversity along with America's past— then you can allay any lingering doubts or fears about the value of independently-produced multicultural videos for you as a teacher and historian.

Copyright ©1992 Deirdre Boyle

FURTHER READING:

Erik Barnouw, *Documentary: The History of Nonfiction Film*, 3rd edition, New York: Oxford University Press, provides a fine introduction to the art and history of documentary film.

Robert A. Rosenstone, "History in Images/History in Words: Reflections on the Possibility of Putting History onto Film," *American Historical Review*, v. 93, no. 5 (December 1988), p.1173-1185, considers the relationship of history and film to the teaching of history.

William Greaves on location, courtesy of the filmmaker

Voice of the *Griot*

AFRICAN-AMERICAN FILM AND VIDEO

Cheryl Chisholm

frican-American film and videomakers can often be heard comparing themselves to the *griot* of African tradition. And many, in forms either subtle or bold, have established a practice of media production that is true to this inspiration.

Who is a *griot*? What does a *griot* do? In most groups indigenous to the African continent, the *griot* is the one-who-remembers, the designated historian, we might say in this context. He or she does not exist at the margins of the group as a scholar or artist, but is firmly ensconced at the center with all others who perform roles of significance for the group. The *griot* announces births and betrothals, as well as deaths and defeats. The *griot* praises, celebrates, mourns, and castigates. The *griot* sings, chants, dramatizes, and editorializes. The *griot* improvises among the requirements of ritual and tradition, contemporary social and economic realities, and the imperatives of his or her own gifts, insight, and style.

This designated historian not only remembers the past, but also communicates and articulates these memories for the group. The *griot* keeps the past alive in the minds and hearts of the group and, in the shaping of the recitation, the consensus of the group about its own identity evolves through time. The *griot* comments on the past in the light of the present, and vice versa, communicating not in the disengaged, third-person voice that has been the hallmark of conventional Western history, but in a manner fully engaged with the ongoing drama of the group. The *griot* is indeed the group's historian and much more, for there is no separation between recording (in this case memorizing) the facts—dates, incidents, personalities—and broadcasting the ever-evolving consensus

The historical and cultural traditions of African American people have become a significant subject in scholarly and popular print and in film and video, thus introducing new and essential information into our understanding of the African-American experience. Not only is the information new, but the ways in which it is expressed are new, as well—personally engaged and, most notably, told in a passionate voice. This voice is not singular but multiple, not simple but complicated by the social and economic dynamics of four hundred years of becoming African American. (Contradictions of color, gender, and class are operative in the history of African Americans, and our voices manifest this, too.)

African-American independent filmmaking, which began in the 1920s and increased following World War II, began to come into full flower in the 1960s. For many African-American filmmakers, the agenda was very specific: to make visible that which had been invisible. Black audiences hungered for recognizable images of themselves, their heroes and heroines, their place in history, their cultural contributions. Some had a sense of what was missing. They had read the available literature; they had paid respectful attention to the stories of the old folks. Many others, however, did not have resources for countering the prevailing myth perpetuated by the dominant culture, that African Americans had no history or culture. They believed, therefore, that they were struggling "up from nothing."

In order to counter such historical distortions, African-American filmmakers felt that audiences needed to have placed, before their very eyes, evidence of the history of a people whose culture continued to be powerful and productive despite appalling conditions of oppression and exclusion. Their priority was to give both black and white audiences positive images of creative and heroic black people on the screen, in order to turn around years of invisibility, ignorance, and neglect. The subjects of these films—black athletes, courageous leaders, and notable cultural

figures—were often chosen to counter prevailing negative notions, and there was a subtle tone of affirmation.

But many of those early filmmakers seemed to downplay their own points of view as they reinscribed the faces of their forebears on the national screen. This was partly a reflection of the neutral, "objective" style of documentary filmmaking which was considered the professional standard at the time. But it was also a classic response to oppression: the newly empowered, unused to their own voices, hesitate to speak too loudly. There is, however, an inherent contradiction in trying to make the formerly invisible visible and to give the voiceless a voice, while at the same time suppressing one's own voice.

By the 1960s African Americans, led by poets, preachers, and politicians, were coming to recognize and love their voices and to understand that "voice" is just another way of saying "point of view" or "way of seeing." It became clear that those traditional ways of making films reflected a world view from which African Americans had been excluded, and were not appropriate for presenting African-American voices in their fullness. To simply include African Americans within the old world view was not sufficient: new structures, capable of manifesting African-American subjectivity, were required. Considerable rethinking and retooling were needed to produce not simply positive and oppositional images, but films that would transform the very terms in which African-American experiences are expressed.

It is no accident that as African-American voices, along with others that historically have been excluded from the national discourse, made themselves heard, the contradictions of mainstream thinking became more evident. The claims of social science to a neutral, objective universality—which, in fact, excludes many realities and points of view—have increasingly come into question. Similarly, claims to an "objectivity" which conceals its own subjectivities, and to "disinterestedness" which hides vested interests, are being challenged. In a culture founded on difference but denying it, the coming into voice of multiple subjectivities requires more than a simple insertion of information that was previously excluded. The whole itself must be reconceived from multiple points of view. And points of view are articulated in what we call "voice."

Image without voice is just another form of blackface. Images do not explain themselves, or clearly represent single meanings. The image slides, like all signifiers, over a chaotic sea of meanings. A given image can signify one thing in one culture and another thing in another culture. It is possible in a multivocal, heterogeneous society such as late twentieth-century America, for a skillfully-edited montage of images to communicate dramatically different, even opposed, meanings to different audiences. It happens all the time, especially in television. One has only to remember the controversy over "All in the Family" or, earlier, "Amos 'n' Andy." In fact, this potential for multiple readings is one of the hallmarks of mass audience appeal.

Word and image must work together to create meanings. In film terms, voice is the construction of point of view through countless choices the filmmaker makes. In a visual/aural text, camera style, film stock, lighting, narrative structure, archival material, music, voice-over, and editing style work together to create "voice." Many contemporary filmmakers are giving renewed attention to the soundtrack and to the possibilities inherent in the interplay between the visual and aural—magnification, subversion, contradiction, irony, congruence—when the soundtrack is imagined as more than mood music or didactic narrative which simply tells you what you are seeing. Voice is generated (or masked) by the imaginative use of all aspects of the production process and of narrative aesthetics.

Eye-witness testimony is one way African-American filmmakers are constructing voice. Two excellent examples of this are THE MASSACHUSETTS 54TH COLORED INFANTRY by Jacqueline Shearer and FREEDOM BAGS by Stanley Nelson. In THE MASSACHUSETTS 54TH COLORED INFANTRY, Shearer makes copious use of interviews with living descendants of members of the regiment. They tell the stories and share the artifacts passed down to them, constantly using the word "we." The unselfconscious use of the first-person plural does more to construct the voice of the film than anything else in its narrative structure. Voice is also constructed in the use of a broad range of African-American music throughout. In subtle ways this film counters the tendency in public television programming to establish a more generic voice.

FREEDOM BAGS presents the first-person histories of several women who

came to Washington, D.C. from the South in hopes of economic prosperity and, instead, found jobs cleaning other people's homes. Their stories of what happened, and how they felt about it, bring to life a period which is usually delineated with statistics.

The issue of voice is most beautifully illustrated in TONGUES UNTIED (see "Crossing Boundaries" section), Marlon Riggs' award-winning and highly controversial videotape. This film about gay black manhood is explicitly about coming into voice, and it uses an extraordinary range of visual devices and aural strategies to build a powerful narrative structure.

Riggs is not the only contemporary filmmaker to use voice-over narration in groundbreaking ways. The use of the familiar newsreel-style voice-over narrator—white, male, and middle-class, judging by his accent—has long been dismissed by many as lazy filmmaking. But several African-American filmmakers have used voice-over narration to powerful effect. Louis Massiah's THE BOMBING OF OSAGE AVENUE is an example. This video is narrated by author Toni Cade Bambara. We never see her and she never employs the first-person singular or plural, but her words and her tone create an intimate space appropriate for hearing the heartbreaking stories told by residents of a bombed-out Philadelphia neighborhood. Bambara, in true *griot* style, gives an intimate history of a place—across time, across ethnic groups, across race and class divisions—which is rare in American media. In this video, "voice" is constructed from voice-over, television news footage of the event, and interviews of great psychological depth.

DIDN'T WE RAMBLE ON is also notable for its use of the voice-over narrator. Filmmaker Billy Jackson made the eccentric and, I think, inspired choice of Dizzy Gillespie as narrator. An authority on African-American music and a man whose well-muscled mouth is made for horn playing, not talking, Gillespie's slow and clearly-mumbled style adds great depth to this precisely and dynamically edited short work. The voice of the film reaches us from inside the history of black music; Gillespie's narrative reads as testimony from one who was there.

One of the more interesting problems for the *griot* who wishes to work in film or video is an obvious one: you need visual images. However, when dealing with historical subjects, images are not always available. A good example is William Greaves' IDA B. WELLS: A PASSION FOR JUSTICE. Ida B. Wells (1862-1931) was a journalist (really an investigative reporter of the most intrepid sort) and an activist. She led an anti-lynching crusade in the United States and Europe, raised a family, and caucused and argued with other African-American leaders of her day. She wrote articles, editorials, pamphlets, and a biography, but there are only a handful of photographs of her in existence. What is a filmmaker to do? William Greaves' solution was to compile drawings and photos of the period and to present author Toni Morrison both as an on-screen presence and in voice-over, reading from Wells' work.

This creates a compelling introduction to Wells' life and work, although it cannot achieve the intimacy we find in a film like JAMES BALDWIN: THE PRICE OF THE TICKET. Here the filmmakers were blessed not only with Baldwin's books and essays but also with stacks of still photographs and miles of moving-image footage from all over the world. Baldwin lived in the media age and was skilled in using film and television to communicate his messages. The voice of this film, through the grace of carefully preserved materials and a skillful editor, is James Baldwin's. There is a warm but ghostly effect, as if Baldwin were speaking to us from beyond the grave, as directly as he speaks in his books.

The voice of the *griot* may be embedded in cultural traditions, but independent film and video is created within the cruel political and economic realities of funding, production, and distribution. So, in actuality, these videotapes represent a series of negotiations which shape the work. They cannot be fully understood without an awareness of the people who made them—their race, class, and sex—and the conditions in which they work, their sources of funding and the agendas of the funders, and where and how their work is distributed. This information can often be found in the materials provided by the distributor, in reviews, and in journals such as the ones listed in the "Alternative Media Resources" section of this volume.

History is a story the *griot* tells. History on film is many stories many *griots* tell. These are evolving stories, representations constructed in an ongoing historical process. Explore these films as sources and as historiography, case studies of history being made before your eyes.

SELECTED INDEPENDENT VIDEOS
AFRICAN AMERICAN

**THE BOMBING OF
OSAGE AVENUE**

Louis J. Massiah 1986

58 min.

Scribe Video Center

On Mothers' Day in 1985 law enforcement officials, police, and firemen, acting under the orders of
Philadelphia's first black mayor, began a tactical assault
on a house occupied by members of a group calling itself
MOVE. THE BOMBING OF OSAGE AVENUE examines
the events leading up to the city's assault and its consequences: 11 people (including children) dead, 61 homes
in charred ruins, 250 people displaced, and an entire city
block destroyed. Longtime residents reflect on the history of their stable middle-class black community; the
impact of MOVE's unconventional lifestyle, which threatened the serenity of their community; and the negligence
of city agencies and officials in addressing their civic-
minded complaints about MOVE's garbage, loudspeak-
ers, and numerous incidents of harassment.

    Set against the backdrop of other historical acts of
violence against black communities in Philadelphia and
other cities, this story reveals how a once tightly-knit
neighborhood became a victim of police violence and
was shattered in the process.

COLOR ADJUSTMENT

Marlon Riggs 1991

87 min.

California Newsreel

Marlon Riggs takes his examination of the stereotyping of
African Americans to prime-time television in this comprehensive documentary. Divided into two parts, the
program combines commentary by scholars, actors, and
producers with clips from prime-time series to develop
an in-depth analysis of stereotypes and the underlying social and economic forces that shape them.

Part I: *Color Blind TV?* (1948-1968) explores the rise of
the new medium and the pervasive role it came to play in
post-war American society. Riggs probes the growing
disparity between the world of the sitcom and the realities of the civil rights movement, juxtaposing clips from
prime-time series such as "Beulah" with footage from network news shows. Scholars and television industry pro-
fessionals, both black and white, explore the relationship

of the African-American community to this new medium, the strategies employed to challenge the prevailing images in such shows as "I Spy," and the inherent limitations of the new prime-time images of African Americans.

Part II: *Coloring the Dream* (1968-1991) focuses on prime-time television as a barometer of the social commitment to changing racial attitudes. Ground-breaking shows, such as "Good Times," are analyzed both for their departure from the traditional television stereotypes and in terms of how their distinctive qualities were eroded or erased over time, in favor of those traditional representations. From "Roots" to "The Cosby Show," Riggs illuminates the relationship between television images and the social and political climate of their times, always in view of the role the television industry has defined for itself in American society.

DIDN'T WE RAMBLE ON

Billy Jackson 1989

14 min.

Filmakers Library

Jazz great Dizzy Gillespie narrates this succinct documentary exploration of the roots and evolution of African rhythm, music, and dance and their influence on African-American culture. DIDN'T WE RAMBLE ON illustrates how elements of the celebratory processions of the Yoruba Egungun masqueraders, which date back seven hundred years, reverberate in the performances of the Florida A&M University Marching Band and jazz funeral processions in New Orleans.

Utilizing archival photos and prints, the video also highlights the ways in which African traditions—ceremonial formations, dress, and regalia—were adapted by military bands in both Europe and colonial America. This material summarizes ten years of research by noted ethnomusicologists.

ETHNIC NOTIONS

Marlon Riggs 1986

56 min.

California Newsreel

This video explores how a variety of stereotypes of African American people have been created and perpetuated in mainstream American culture, and how those stereotypes serve social and political purposes. Many common stereotypes, such as "Toms, Sambos, Coons, Mammies, Pickaninnies, and Brutes"—and their manifestations in popular culture—are illustrated in theatre, song, and film excerpts.

The visual core of the videotape is a collection of black memorabilia and artifacts such as greeting cards, advertisements, cartoons, feature films, children's games, and household objects. Scholars including Lawrence Levine, Barbara Christian, and Patricia Turner comment on the ways in which these stereotypical images have been used in an attempt to resolve the social contradictions engendered by the existence of slavery and racism in a democratic society. Pre-Civil War images of singing, dancing, "contented" slaves, for instance, implied that slavery was a benign institution. Conversely, portrayals of black men as brutish and sexually predatory both incited and were used to justify violence against African Americans following Reconstruction.

While stereotypes may be historically specific, their persisting characteristics may be observed as well. The Mammy, for instance—the image of a desexualized woman who presumably finds her fulfillment in serving white families—first appeared during the period of slavery and, with small changes, continues to be seen on commercial products and television today.

An accompanying study guide is available with ETHNIC NOTIONS. See also COLOR ADJUSTMENT, which considers many of these issues in television programming.

EYES ON THE PRIZE: AMERICA'S CIVIL RIGHTS YEARS, 1954 TO 1965

Henry Hampton,

Executive Producer 1986

6-part series

60 min. each

PBS Video

This landmark series traces the birth and evolution of the civil rights movement in America. Covering the period from 1954 through 1965, these six programs present in-depth coverage of the social, political, and economic conditions that impelled African Americans' nationwide campaign for equal rights and equal justice under the law. The series is comprised of media records from the time: news footage, photographs, and interviews with people, both black and white, involved in every level of the movement.

AWAKENINGS (1954-1956)—*Brown v. Board of Education of Topeka, Kansas;* black freedom movement begins in the South; the lynching of Emmett Till; the psychology of segregation; Rosa Parks sparks the Montgomery bus boycott; the emerging leadership of Rev. Martin Luther King, Jr.

and the formation of the Southern Christian Leadership Conference (SCLC).

FIGHTING BACK (1957-1962)—the struggle to integrate public schools; nine black students enter Little Rock, Arkansas, Central High School; James Meredith attempts to enroll in the University of Mississippi.

AIN'T SCARED OF YOUR JAILS (1960-1961)—individuals and groups challenge racial injustice; Federal awareness of the civil rights movement; student organizing leads to the formation of the Student Nonviolent Coordinating Committee (SNCC); tactics of civil disobedience include sit-ins and freedom rides.

NO EASY WALK (1962-1966)—growing commitment to the strategy of nonviolence; demonstrations and marches in Albany, Georgia; Birmingham, Alabama; and Washington, D.C.

MISSISSIPPI: IS THIS AMERICA? (1962-1964)—Freedom Summer '64; Northern civil rights workers mobilize to work with SNCC on voters' rights campaigns; the murders of Michael Schwerner, Andrew Goodman, and James Chaney.

BRIDGE TO FREEDOM (1965)—Rev. Martin Luther King, Jr. receives the Nobel Peace Prize; strategies of nonviolence challenged; the pivotal march from Selma to Montgomery, Alabama; the Voting Rights Bill is signed by President Lyndon Johnson; the civil rights movement begins to broaden its social agenda, having achieved significant legal aims.

This series is accompanied by a study guide, an anthology of readings, and a companion volume.

EYES ON THE PRIZE II: AMERICA AT THE RACIAL CROSSROADS, 1965 TO 1985

Henry Hampton,

Executive Producer 1989

8-part series

60 min. each

PBS Video

This series begins where the first left off, intercutting archival film and television footage with interviews to chart the rise of new political and community leaders; challenges to the strategy of nonviolence; urban unrest across the country; and the murders of key civil rights leaders. (The names of individual program producers follow program titles.)

THE TIME HAS COME (1964-1965), *James A. DeVinney and Madison Davis Lacy, Jr.*—the growing influence of the Nation of Islam in the black community; Malcolm X.

TWO SOCIETIES (1965-1968), *Sheila Bernard and Sam Pollard*—Rev. Martin Luther King, Jr. brings the message of nonviolence north to Chicago; confrontation between police and the black community culminates in violent clashes in Detroit.

POWER! (1967-1968), *Louis J. Massiah and Terry Kay Rockefeller*—Carl Stokes is elected the first black mayor of a major American city; the formation of the Black Panther Party.

THE PROMISED LAND (1967-1968), *Paul Stekler and Jacqueline Shearer*—Rev. Martin Luther King, Jr. publicly denounces the Vietnam War; the F.B.I. intensifies surveillance of civil rights activists; the Poor People's March to Washington; the Memphis sanitation workers' strike; the assassination of Rev. Martin Luther King, Jr.

AIN'T GONNA SHUFFLE NO MORE (1964-1972), *Sam Pollard and Sheila Bernard*—the emergence of the black consciousness movement; renewed interest in African-American arts and popular culture; Cassius Clay adopts the name Muhammad Ali.

A NATION OF LAW? (1968-1971), *Terry Kay Rockefeller, Thomas Ott, and Louis J. Massiah*—Bobby Seale; key Chicago-based Black Panthers are killed in a police raid; the Attica prison revolt in upstate New York.

THE KEYS TO THE KINGDOM (1974-1980), *Jacqueline Shearer and Paul Stekler*—focus on education and employment; black parents in Boston demand equal education for their children; court-ordered school bussing; affirmative action programs instituted; Bakke case challenges affirmative action.

BACK TO THE MOVEMENT (1979-mid 1980s), *Madison Davis Lacy, Jr. and James A. DeVinney*—police brutality and the murder of a black community leader draws attention to racism in Miami; the election of Chicago's first black mayor; a recap of significant moments from the civil rights movement.

A study guide and anthology of readings accompany the series.

FREEDOM BAGS

Elizabeth Clark-Lewis and Stanley Nelson 1990

32 min.

Filmakers Library

FREEDOM BAGS probes an often-overlooked aspect of American labor history, documenting the experiences of African-American women who migrated from the rural South to Washington, D.C. during the first three decades of this century in search of economic opportunities. They discovered, however, that the only "opportunities" available to them were similar to those which they had hoped to escape: domestic service and other low-level positions.

In this video, elderly black women who have spent much of their lives in domestic service recall their initial hopes for a better life, the reality of their low-paying, dead-end jobs, and the community of support they developed with each other. Their reflections, and film and newsreel clips of the period, offer an overview of domestic service during this century and how it facilitated the emergence of Washington's middle class. See also THE MAIDS and MILES OF SMILES for more on the history of black workers in America.

FROM THESE ROOTS

William Greaves 1974

28 min.

William Greaves Productions

This documentary provides a valuable overview of the luminous period in American history known as the Harlem Renaissance. Opening with New York City's rousing 1919 welcome home parade for the men of the Harlem-based 369th Infantry, heralded for their courage in battle, the film details the influx of African Americans into New York's Harlem after World War I. As blacks moved in, whites moved out, and Harlem became a vibrant community where African Americans could live relatively unharassed.

Harlem in the 1920s became a scene of political and cultural rebirth. Artistic activity flourished as African-American writers, photographers, dancers, musicians, and singers flocked in. Through period photographs and archival footage, and with original music by Eubie Blake, the story unfolds through the lives of such notables as Langston Hughes, Countee Cullen and James Weldon Johnson, Ethel Waters and Josephine Baker, W.E.B. Du Bois and Marcus Garvey, Duke Ellington and Eubie Blake, Paul Robeson, James Van DerZee, and a host of others whose literature and music influenced American culture and thought in the 1920s and 1930s. See also I REMEMBER HARLEM and UNCOMMON IMAGES: JAMES VAN DERZEE.

I REMEMBER HARLEM

William Miles 1980

4-part series

58 min. each

Films for the Humanities and Sciences

I REMEMBER HARLEM is a series of four, one-hour programs that survey the diverse cultures which have flourished since 1600 in the area of New York City called Harlem. From Native Americans, Dutch and Irish, Finns and Jews to Italians, African Americans and Latinos, Harlem has been home to an extraordinary social diversity.

THE DEPRESSION YEARS: 1930-1940, Part 2 of the series, recalls the flourishing art and culture of Harlem through interviews with eyewitnesses and archival film, photographs, and audio. The rise of the labor movement and the role of the WPA are featured. The film also discusses the significance of such public figures as Father Divine, who fed the poor and awakened the idealism of the black community, and champion boxer Joe Louis, as symbols of leadership.

TOWARD FREEDOM: 1940-1965, Part 3 of the series, focuses on a period during which African Americans achieved broad integration into the political and economic life of New York City. Harlem, from the Apollo to the U.S.O., was an entertainment mecca during World War II. Performers who rose to prominence during the War and the political and social atmosphere of the post-war period are highlighted.

A study guide for the series is available. See also FROM THESE ROOTS, about the Harlem Renaissance.

IDA B. WELLS:
A PASSION FOR JUSTICE

William Greaves 1989

53 min.

William Greaves Productions

Initially broadcast on "The American Experience" series, this documentary is a biography of Ida B. Wells (1862-1931), investigative reporter, human rights activist, suffragist, and anti-lynching crusader of the late-nineteenth and early-twentieth centuries, who has been all but forgotten in history books. In response to post-Civil War lynchings and segregation, Ida B. Wells became a journalist, publishing editorials, pamphlets, and newspaper articles in the U.S. and England. Her involvement with the suffrage movement and fight for freedom of the press made her a revolutionary voice and spirit, presaging the civil rights, human rights, and women's movements. Wells' position as a black woman working with both the women's movement and the early civil rights movement led her into many debates with her peers, and made her a voice of conscience in both worlds.

Despite the scarcity of photo-documentation of Wells herself, she is brought to life through hundreds of archival photos and interviews with scholars, including her grandson. Most dramatically, author Toni Morrison reads from Wells' spirited writings. The film makes clear Wells' influence on such notable leaders as Frederick Douglass, W.E.B. Du Bois, A. Philip Randolph, Malcolm X, and Rev. Martin Luther King, Jr.

JAMES BALDWIN:
THE PRICE OF THE TICKET

Karen Thorsen and

William Miles 1989

87 min.

California Newsreel

James Baldwin (1924-1987) was one of twentieth-century America's foremost writers and social thinkers. In this biography, Baldwin's experiences as an African American, a man, and a homosexual are explored for their contributions to his unique vision and intellect. Through interviews and, most vividly, his writing, Baldwin is revealed as an artist whose art became his weapon in the search for human rights.

From his childhood in Harlem to his death, James Baldwin lived through some of the most tumultuous events in black-white relations in the United States. In such works as *Notes of a Native Son* and *The Fire Next Time*, Baldwin emerged as a voice that spoke the growing black anger in words that society at large would hear.

Baldwin's international stature as an artist and an intellectual is shown through scenes of his life in France and Morocco. In on-camera interviews, he explains why living in the United States became increasingly difficult for him, and how he needed to live abroad in order to survive as an artist. James Baldwin had a paradoxical ability to draw inspiration from the very social conditions that, ultimately, threatened his ability to create.

A study guide is available.

THE MAIDS

Muriel Jackson 1985

28 min.

Women Make Movies

Utilizing period drawings, photographs, and contemporary oral histories of women who have worked or who continue to work as domestics, THE MAIDS examines domestic work since slavery. Many issues are discussed: the stigma often associated with this type of occupation; the lack of job advancement available to domestic workers; and the formation of the National Domestic Workers' Union and its lobbying efforts to secure for domestic workers the full protection and benefits guaranteed by U.S. labor laws.

This history is contrasted with an examination of predominantly white-owned, entrepreneurial cleaning services, which have become more common in recent years. Their existence validates the importance of domestic work, and their owners are quick to suggest that they have helped to elevate the work to a level of professional respectability, but it also highlights the fact that domestic workers, black and white, continue to work for low wages in dead-end jobs.

See also FREEDOM BAGS.

THE MASSACHUSETTS 54TH COLORED INFANTRY

Jacqueline Shearer 1991

58 min.

PBS Video

During the Civil War 178,975 black men served as soldiers in the Union Army. Filmmaker Jacqueline Shearer has produced a comprehensive yet strikingly intimate account of the men of the first official regiment of Northern black soldiers to fight in the Civil War, the Massachusetts 54th Colored Infantry. Originally aired as part of "The American Experience" series, the documentary presents the story from the viewpoints of the soldiers and their families, and includes oral histories of their descendants. Their accounts reveal a history which is not found in textbooks, but which has been passed down through generations in African-American communities.

THE MASSACHUSETTS 54TH COLORED INFANTRY examines how the black and white abolitionist movement, working to eradicate slavery, also cultivated the seeds of black military service. Focusing on Boston, this film is not only about the ex-slaves but also the laborers, blacksmiths, ministers, farmers, doctors, lawyers, and others from Massachusetts and neighboring states who joined the 54th. These men had to fight first for the right to fight, then for equal pay with white soldiers, and finally against the Confederate Army.

The film places the war experiences of the members of the Massachusetts 54th in a larger social context, and includes information about their families, their unique training, and the long-term effects of their military experience. The film interweaves carefully researched African-American music from the period; photographs; quotes from diaries, letters, speeches, and newspaper articles; scholarly commentary; and filmed oral histories.

MILES OF SMILES, YEARS OF STRUGGLE

Paul Wagner and Jack Santino 1982

58 min.

California Newsreel

This documentary narrated by Rosina Tucker, a union organizer and widow of a porter, chronicles the successful struggle of sleeping car porters to organize the first black trade union. Using interviews with retired porters, archival photographs, film clips, and union songs, it explores the contradictions of porters' lives—a sense of pride in a job well done contrasted with anger over substandard working conditions and the limited job options that were available to blacks at the time. The film describes how the response of the porters to the contradictions of their lives resulted in groundbreaking organizing efforts to form the Brotherhood of Sleeping Car Porters, and then to force the Pullman Company to recognize it. The union, under the visionary leadership of A. Philip Randolph, went on to successfully challenge racial discrimination in the government and defense industries, and was in the forefront of the civil rights movement. In this film, retired porter and activist E.D. Nixon recalls his role in organizing the bus boycott in Montgomery, Alabama, and A. Philip Randolph is seen in his role as a leader of the 1963 civil rights march on Washington.

A PLACE OF RAGE

Pratibha Parmar 1991

52 min.

Women Make Movies

The activist role played by black women in the civil rights movement and their continuing concerns as women of color is highlighted in this video. Poet June Jordan, professor Angela Davis, and author Alice Walker reflect on their early lives as activists during the 1960s and 1970s, paying special respect to the leadership of Rosa Parks and Fanny Lou Hamer. June Jordan reads her poetry, which connects personal history, race, and feminist politics to a larger world view. Angela Davis' controversial history with the Black Panther movement, the Communist Party, and her subsequent listing as the F.B.I.'s "most wanted" woman, is presented in news footage and in her own recollections.

This tape, made by an Asian-Indian British filmmaker, reflects the way in which discussion of racial issues has evolved from polarized black-white scenarios to more polycultural approaches. Alice Walker and filmmaker Trinh T. Minh-ha (see SURNAME VIET GIVEN NAME NAM in the "Crossing Boundaries" section) also discuss the influences on their lives, work, and self-identity as women of color. This traditional documentary about non-traditional women examines the role that African-American women have played in complex situations. See also William Greaves' IDA B. WELLS: A PASSION FOR JUSTICE about an early and influential woman activist.

THE ROAD TO BROWN

Mykola Kulish 1990

47 min.

California Newsreel

The principal focus here is on Charles Hamilton Houston, whose leadership was responsible for the landmark 1954 Supreme Court decision *Brown v. Board of Education of Topeka, Kansas,* which declared segregated education unconstitutional. The scenario intercuts a history of segregation, from the arrival of the first enslaved Africans at Jamestown, Virginia through the passage of Jim Crow laws in 1896, with scenes filmed in the contemporary South.

Charles Hamilton Houston was born in 1895 in Washington, D.C. His mother was a teacher, his father a lawyer. Houston, one of the few blacks to attend Amherst College, went on to become the first African-American editor of the Harvard Law Review, the dean of Howard University Law School, and chief counsel to the NAACP.

This program documents Houston's career and his strategic plans to contest the "separate but equal" doctrine of the Supreme Court's 1896 *Plessy v. Ferguson* decision which sustained segregated education.

Photographs and film footage, shot by Houston as evidence of unequal conditions in black schools, are seen here. Colleagues recall Houston's tireless efforts, which led to the 1954 decision handed down by the Supreme Court four years after his untimely death. This is the little-known story of an unsung African American's fight for racial equality.

TO SLEEP WITH ANGER

Charles Burnett 1990

105 min.

Sony Video Software

Filmmaker Charles Burnett's narrative feature about a middle-class Southern black family living in Los Angeles opens with a common event—the unexpected arrival of an old friend from the South—but evolves into a subtle and disturbing clash of cultures and values. On the surface, visitor Harry Mention (Danny Glover) is a charming if sometimes demanding guest who entertains family members and neighbors with his jokes and tales of folklore and magic. But a more dangerous dynamic becomes apparent, at least to the woman of the house, which will ultimately threaten not just the family's comfortable lifestyle, but the very lives of its members.

In this nuanced family drama, Burnett explores a significant theme in American history: the shift from a rural culture to an urban environment, with the loss of sustaining personal and spiritual traditions. In his choice of Harry Mention as the dramatic catalyst, Burnett reaches back into traditional African myth for the Trickster figure, and acknowledges the importance of the oral tradition in African-American culture.

TROUBLE BEHIND

Robbie Henson 1990

56 min.

California Newsreel

This is a view of the social mechanisms of racism from the point of view of a white filmmaker. It focuses on the town of Corbin, Kentucky, which—in 1919—expelled its black residents, most of whom had migrated to Corbin as railroad workers during World War I. While this event is not featured in the town's official history, it has had far-reaching consequences that can still be felt today. More than seventy years later, Corbin is a white town, largely because the few blacks who have ventured to make their homes there have been made unwelcome.

Filmmaker Robbie Henson, who grew up not far from Corbin, returned to the town to see what impact its racial history and isolation has had on the attitudes of the residents. The first part of the film examines the 1919 episode, intercutting oral histories of current Corbin residents and black residents of neighboring towns with newspaper accounts and scholarly research. The second part of the film examines current racial attitudes in Corbin through interviews with a variety of residents, young and old. Older residents deny negative racial attitudes, while teenagers freely express virulent opinions. An African-American historian speaks of cross-burnings and other acts of violence against blacks who have attempted to settle in the town. The film provides a personal view of the legacy of racism, spoken and unspoken, in an American community.

TWO DOLLARS AND A DREAM

Stanley Nelson 1987

56 min.

Filmakers Library

This biography of the first African-American woman millionaire, Madame C.J. Walker, is a matter-of-fact description of Madame Walker's accomplishments and legacy. The daughter of freed slaves, Sarah Breedlove Walker (1867-1919) founded the Madame C.J. Walker Company in Indianapolis in 1901. The business was based on her patented invention—a hot comb—and a line of hair care and beauty products sold by and to African-American women in their homes (a precursor to Mary Kay and Avon cosmetic sales systems). With her factory production, beauty colleges, and allied business enterprises, Madame Walker created a complex economic organization which emphasized advancement for women. Although some of her products—such as hair straighteners and skin lighteners—were criticized as attempts to replicate white beauty culture, Marcus Garvey praised her for providing jobs for 3,000 African Americans.

Except for her lawyer, all of her employees were black women, some of whom appear here recalling their experiences with Madame Walker. The employment of African-American women in managerial, sales, secretarial, and promotion jobs was revolutionary for its time. Walker contributed generously to the black community and to charities during her lifetime. She left the bulk of her fortune to her daughter, A'Leilia, who became an arts patron during the Harlem Renaissance in New York.

Nelson incorporates rare old photographs, hand-colored slides, and company promotional materials to create a vivid profile.

ALSO RECOMMENDED:

ADAM CLAYTON POWELL, Richard Kilberg and Yvonne Smith 1989, 53 min., Direct Cinema Limited
This film focuses on the complex and controversial political career and personal life of Adam Clayton Powell. Pastor of America's largest Protestant congregation, and one of the country's most influential congressmen, his longtime advocacy for federal civil rights laws was realized in landmark legislation in the 1960s.

FLAG, Linda Gibson 1989, 24 min., Women Make Movies
A personal meditation on growing up black and female in the 1950s becomes the occasion for considering the dilemmas of being patriotic in a racist society. Gibson uses childhood diaries and school and family photos, as well as collage and interpretive dance, to chart her evolving awareness.

GOTTA MAKE THIS JOURNEY: SWEET HONEY IN THE ROCK, Michelle Parkerson 1983, 58 min., Women Make Movies
A profile of the *a capella* activist singing group, Sweet Honey in the Rock. Group founder and musicologist Bernice Reagon explains the vital role of music as a bearer of historical information in African-American culture. Concert footage is intercut with interviews with group members to capture their unique style which blends gospel, folk, soul, and African musical traditions.

LANGSTON HUGHES: THE DREAM KEEPER, St. Clair Bourne 1986, 60 min., Annenberg/CPB Project
This richly-textured portrait of a gifted author includes archival film footage, interviews with friends and associates, and readings from Langston Hughes' work, to evoke the range and power of his literary and political contributions. Blues and spoken poetry are part of a complex soundtrack that evokes Hughes' subjective voice and point of view.

THE LEGACY OF ARTURO ALFONSO SCHOMBURG, Angela Fontanez 1986, 27 min., WNYC-TV
This docudrama depicts the life and work of Puerto Rican bibliophile Arthur Schomburg, who throughout his life collected books and artifacts documenting the

history of people of African descent. His extensive collection forms the basis of the New York Public Library's Arthur Schomburg Center for Research in Black Culture.

ROOTS OF RESISTANCE: A STORY OF THE UNDERGROUND RAILROAD, Orlando Bagwell 1990, 60 min., PBS Video

In the mid-1800s, a network of escape routes known as the underground railroad offered black men and women their only hope of obtaining freedom from slavery. Using the narratives of escaped slaves, this film tells the story of ex-slaves, suffragists, and abolitionists who, at great personal risk, assisted slaves to freedom.

UNCOMMON IMAGES: JAMES VAN DERZEE, Evelyn Barron 1978, 22 min., Filmakers Library

A portrait of a major American photographer who was one of the foremost chroniclers of Harlem's black community. Van DerZee's work is abundantly represented in this film, complemented by interviews with the photographer.

Family Gathering, courtesy of the filmmaker

Intimate Histories

ASIAN-AMERICAN FILM AND VIDEO

Daryl Chin

sian-American independent video is part of a larger effort by underrepresented groups to reexamine and retell U.S. history. The term "Asian American" itself is strategic, having been taken up by political activists in the 1960s to replace the term "Oriental," with its connotations of exoticism and otherness. The term today embraces a diversity of ethnicities and nationalities, from Chinese-American to Pakistani-American. Such self-identification has provided a way of retaining connections with our disparate heritages, while claiming a place in the larger American society.

Any attempt to chart Asian-American history is complicated by the irregular patterns of immigration and assimilation of different groups. Although there has been Asian immigration to the United States since the period after the Civil War, it was severely limited until the passage of new immigration laws in the mid-1960s. The influx of new immigrants that followed has produced a diversity of Asian cultures in the United States.

Asian-American independent media speaks to these diverse experiences. It also documents a history that has been overlooked, suppressed, and misrepresented. These films and videotapes humanize the experiences of immigration and cultural assimilation; they reveal how people's lives are affected by historical events; they show how American culture is continually evolving. Christine Choy's FROM SPIKES TO SPINDLES, a documentary about garment workers on New York's Lower East Side, for example, uses interviews with workers to depict the oppressive conditions under which Asian immigrants have worked. Felicia Lowe's CARVED IN SILENCE, about the Angel Island detention center, weaves together letters, interviews, photographs, and other memorabilia to summon the voices of Chinese immigrants seeking to enter California between 1882 and 1943.

The Japanese-American internment has been the subject of a significant group of documentaries, ranging from the straight-forward objectivity of UNFINISHED BUSINESS to the more poetic HISTORY AND MEMORY. These independent works, many of them based on extensive original research, make powerful use of documentary evidence, personal memory, and artifacts in their search for a suppressed past.

The internment not only deprived a group of American citizens of their constitutional rights (the majority of those interned were born in the United States), it also raised issues of racism. The assumption that non-whites would be more apt to betray the United States than whites (of German and Italian ancestry, for example), an idea disproved by F.B.I. reports recently released through the Freedom of Information Act, lay at the heart of the internment policy.

Congressional hearings on redress for Japanese-Americans interned during World War II, which established the culpability of the United States government in depriving its own citizens of rights and property, were held in the mid-1980s. The hearings stimulated a reappraisal of the internment in which independent filmmakers played an active role. These productions make important contributions to the historical record. And, in contrast to the conventions of mainstream media, they tell their stories from Japanese-American perspectives.

A film such as COME SEE THE PARADISE is a good example of a familiar Hollywood approach. While internment is the subject of the film, the focus is not on Japanese-Americans, but on a white outsider who is married to a Japanese-American woman. It is his story. This has the effect of distancing the internment experience as something that happened to "others." It would be illuminating to show COME SEE THE PARADISE in conjunction with one of the independent works on the list,

and ask students to compare how each one tells its story, how points of view are constructed, and how visual images are used to convey information and mood.

Steven Okazaki's UNFINISHED BUSINESS—one of the first documentaries on the internment experience from the point of view of Japanese-Americans—centers on the accounts of three men who testified at the Congressional hearings. The film intercuts personal interviews with the three men, who reveal how internment affected their lives, with their Congressional testimony. Skillfully combining photographs, commentary, and archival footage, Okazaki conveys a sense of the personal consequences of the upheavals of World War II. UNFINISHED BUSINESS was especially important at the time it was made, because it broke a long silence: Japanese-American families, feeling shame at their imprisonment, had rarely discussed this period of their lives.

Lise Yasui, the niece of one of the men profiled in UNFINISHED BUSINESS, set out to break a silence in her own family history. Her documentary, FAMILY GATHERING, uses an intimate approach to unearth a personal past. She grew up in the 1950s and 1960s hearing relatively little about her family's internment experience. Yasui interweaves home movies, family reminiscences, and personal voice as she pursues an investigation into her family's hidden history. Her film provides a powerful sense of how social and personal history intersect.

The process of searching for the past is also the subject of video artist Rea Tajiri's HISTORY AND MEMORY. Tajiri's work has a three-part vision: first, a documentary approach using archival material; second, a media analysis of visual imagery—including Hollywood movies, news photos, magazines—that shapes historical memory and cultural identity; and family memories, for which there are no pictures and which therefore are seen only in the imagination. Tajiri's videotape, like many other works on internment, calls attention to a sense of amnesia in many Japanese-American families in the face of a past too painful and traumatic to recall. This absence of memory is mirrored in the absence of family records, photographs, letters, and books—much of which was lost or destroyed in the process of relocation.

Students might be asked to consider ways in which available evidence affects our understanding of the past, and what strategies can be used to critically interpret the evidence which is available. Tajiri searches through official documents, Hollywood movies, government propaganda films, snapshots, and personal stories in her quest for the truth of the past. She shows how images can be created, retrieved, and interpreted to produce an historical record and correct historical imbalances.

Unlike the fictional COME SEE THE PARADISE, films like HISTORY AND MEMORY, FAMILY GATHERING, and UNFINISHED BUSINESS do not emphasize romance or emotional catharsis. Instead, viewers are challenged to confront their preconceptions...and their discomfort.

FORBIDDEN CITY, U.S.A. reveals another aspect of Asian-American history: not a story of immigration, not a story of the search for cultural identity, but a story of assimilation to mainstream American culture. This film, by Arthur Dong, introduces a group of highly articulate, engaging, and totally Americanized entertainers—Japanese-Americans, Filipino-Americans, and Chinese-Americans—who dreamed of careers in show business in the 1940s despite the prejudicial hiring practices common in the entertainment industry. As the performers point out, their desire to work as entertainers evoked the incredulity of many white club owners, the shock of their traditional Chinese and Japanese elders, and casual but constant discrimination.

The opening of the Forbidden City nightclub in San Francisco offered these performers an opportunity to realize their aspirations. Some of them talk about travelling in the segregated South during the 1940s and 1950s, occupying an anomalous position in a world of "whites only" and "blacks only." One woman explains how, while travelling in the Midwest, she was approached by someone who was very excited to see an "Oriental" and asked if she understood English. Her response was, "Not a damn word!" Students can contrast the stereotyped characters that Asian-American actors have been forced to play in movie and television roles, with the people encountered in this film.

The prototypical American experiences of immigration, of attempting to maintain cultural traditions in a new environment, and experiencing the tensions of assimilation, have been played in many variations in Asian-American independent media. Mira Nair's SO FAR FROM INDIA follows the daily routine of a recent

immigrant from India who has left wife and family behind in order to establish himself in New York City. His sense of freedom is balanced by an acute sense of displacement and loneliness. The awkwardness he feels upon a return visit to India makes the conflicting emotions of this family saga palpable.

The opposing demands of traditional values and assimilation continue to present dilemmas. Asian-American women, in particular, have felt pressure to conform to dominant stereotypes of beauty and social behavior. This conflict is examined in Pam Tom's narrative short, TWO LIES. This video, which is about a Chinese-American woman who attempts to assimilate by having an operation to make her eyes appear "rounder," shows the personal costs of cultural denial. Valerie Soe's brief videotape, ALL ORIENTALS LOOK THE SAME, in which several Asian-American faces are shown in a series of dissolves, effectively gives the lie to its title.

Independent works like these serve a dual function: they reinforce a sense of shared experience among Asian Americans of diverse backgrounds; they also inform and enrich the larger society with authentic Asian-American voices and viewpoints. Many of the titles listed in this guide were produced by people working within a network of Asian-American media centers that foster both production and distribution of independent media. These media centers include Visual Communications in Los Angeles, Asian CineVision in New York City, and the National Asian American Telecommunications Association in San Francisco. (See the "Alternative Media Resources" section). In addition to these specifically Asian-American organizations, documentary production organizations such as Third World Newsreel, Film News Now, and Downtown Community Television have also provided distribution services for Asian-American producers.

While media centers are not the only means for producing Asian-American film and video, they have provided an important context for exhibiting and disseminating works with specifically Asian-American perspectives. Arthur Dong's CLAIMING A VOICE, an affectionate documentary celebrating the twentieth anniversary of Visual Communications, introduces personalities, projects, and presentations of this organization. It shows how an important body of work has been created by a community of media makers.

Documentary film producer Renee Tajima has written, "The greatest achievement of the Asian-American documentary may be its intimacy." At their best, these Asian-American films and videos apply personal perspectives to historical events, thereby encouraging an empathetic response in the viewer. What follows is only a selective sampling of the independent productions available for teaching. They provide a vivid record of lived history and reveal the human dimensions of racism, assimilation, and cultural identity in American society.

FURTHER READING:

The Asian American Media Reference Guide. Bernice Chu, editor; Bill Gee, editor, revised edition. New York: Asian CineVision, 1986; 1991.

Moving the Image: Independent Asian Pacific American Media Arts. Russell Leong, editor. Los Angeles: UCLA Asian American Studies Center and Visual Communications, 1991.

SELECTED INDEPENDENT VIDEOS
ASIAN AMERICAN

ALL ORIENTALS LOOK THE SAME

Valerie Soe 1986

1 min.

Women Make Movies

This brief experimental videotape is a witty and telling critique of racial stereotyping. To show the fallacy of her title, Ms. Soe, a fourth-generation Chinese-American, presents a rapid-fire series of individual head shots of Asian Americans. Male and female, young and old, her subjects share Asian roots, but they do not look the same. This videotape can be a catalyst for discussion about racial stereotyping and its pervasiveness. See also ETHNIC NOTIONS for a look at the issue of stereotyping.

CARVED IN SILENCE

Felicia Lowe 1987

45 min.

CrossCurrent Media

Early Chinese immigrants to the U.S. mined minerals, reclaimed land for agricultural use, and built railroads. But in 1882, the Chinese Exclusion Act was passed: for the first time in U.S. history, immigrants were excluded solely on the basis of race. This documentary looks at the immigration station at Angel Island, a small island in San

Francisco Bay. At this "Ellis Island of the West," Chinese immigrants seeking entry into the U.S. were confined in barracks packed with triple-tier bunks for one to two hundred men, and subjected to relentless questioning. Detainees faced a ten-month to two-year detention. One slip-up or "wrong answer" about their family or life in China could lead to deportation. Recollections of former detainees, some of whom were initially deported and returned to try again, and dramatized segments, portray the dehumanizing treatment endured by these immigrants. President Franklin D. Roosevelt repealed the Chinese Exclusion Act in 1943 as a wartime gesture to our ally, China, but the legacy of racial exclusion had profound long-term effects for Chinese-Americans.

Angel Island is now a park; but the poems of hope and pain which remain, carved by Chinese immigrants into its wooden barracks walls, are movingly documented in this evocation of a dark period in our immigration history.

CLAIMING A VOICE

Arthur Dong 1990

60 min.

Visual Communications;

DeepFocus

The importance of independent media to Asian-American cultural identity is clearly documented in CLAIMING A VOICE, which details the twenty-year history of Visual Communications, the first group dedicated to producing and promoting media made by and about Asian-Pacific Americans. Directed by Arthur Dong, (see his SEWING WOMAN and FORBIDDEN CITY, U.S.A.), the documentary introduces V.C.'s original movers and shakers, young people whose consciousness was raised during their college years in the counterculture 1960s. Excluded from film industry or arts-related jobs which were closed to Asian Americans at that time, the young V.C. founders (many of them graduates of the UCLA film school) decided to form a democratically-run production organization dedicated to creating positive images of Asians in cinema and teaching other Asian Americans to use media to empower their communities.

Generously highlighted with clips from V.C. shorts, features, and children's media produced by staff members and their students, CLAIMING A VOICE tracks the rocky road of the nonprofit organization from its years as an active production facility in the 1970s, through its evolution into a media arts organization focused on production support, media education and advocacy, and community outreach (see "Alternative Media Resources" section). The history of Visual Communications is, in effect, the history of a body of Asian-American media work that helped create a new frame of reference, replacing media stereotypes with positive, culturally authentic depictions.

See also STARTING FIRE WITH GUNPOWDER ("Native American" section) about how the Inuit Broadcasting Corporation counters stereotypes and advances cultural values.

DAYS OF WAITING

Steven Okazaki 1990

28 min.

Mouchette Films;

CrossCurrent Media

This film details life inside Japanese-American internment camps as it was experienced by an outsider. Artist Estelle Peck Ishigo was the Caucasian wife of a Japanese-American husband. In a dramatic voice-over narrative in the form of a letter to a fellow camp internee, she recalls the atmosphere of racism in California in the 1930s (where interracial marriages could not be performed) and the joy she felt upon being welcomed into her husband's Japanese-American community.

When Japanese-Americans were sent to relocation camps after Pearl Harbor, Ishigo accompanied her husband into four years of internment. She was one of a handful of Caucasians in the camps. Here, through her letters and drawings, paintings and photographs, we have a personal and detailed view of the lives of people during internment. Accepted without question or prejudice by fellow internees, Ishigo was determined to survive and help others survive with dignity. She organized a camp newspaper, played in the camp band, and documented camp life in her art work and photography.

This tragic and moving story of personal fortitude does not end with the Ishigos' release from internment. Poverty, illness, and hardship continued to plague them. Estelle Ishigo's art work, personal papers, and memories were recorded before her death by filmmaker Okazaki, a third-generation Japanese-American, to provide a unique and revealing testament. See also Okazaki's UNFINISHED BUSINESS.

EIGHT-POUND LIVELIHOOD

Yuet-Fung Ho 1984

27 min.

New York Chinatown History Project

Archival and family photos and personal reminiscences from first-and second-generation Chinese-Americans recreate the story of Chinese laundry workers in America, and how their occupation affected their family life and the future lives of their children. Interviews with non-Chinese New Yorkers also reveal common misconceptions about how and why Chinese immigrants ran laundries. Long hours, backbreaking labor (the irons alone weighed eight pounds apiece), and customer abuse are some of the harsh realities of this trade that Chinese immigrants were forced to create for themselves when they were banned from most other occupations.

While dignity and pride in a job well done infuse the elders' commentary, two adult children of Chinese launderers recall the details of daily life in cramped quarters and tell a different story. Having become artists whose music and writing reflects their cultural roots, these two young people remember, with a suggestion of their anger and bitterness, what it was like to grow up in a Chinese laundry. See also FROM SPIKES TO SPINDLES for an account of Chinese immigrant labor in America.

FAMILY GATHERING

Lise Yasui and Ann Tegnell 1988

30 min.

New Day Films

A deeply personal inquiry into the meaning of the Japanese-American internment as it affected one family. Filmmaker Lise Yasui, the daughter of a Japanese-American physician father and a Caucasian mother, goes back fifty years through three generations of her father's family which, prior to Pearl Harbor, held a position of respect in an Oregon community. In her attempt to understand her family history and her place in it, she confronts hidden family trauma and tragedy as well as the larger issues of civil rights, prejudice, and discrimination.

Yasui's grandfather, a prominent shopkeeper and orchard farmer, is the film's central focus, for as a community leader he was the first targeted for official suspicion. Accused of spying for Japan and of plotting to blow up the Panama Canal (the F.B.I. found crude maps of the Canal in his house, a school project done by one of his children), he was held in detention for the duration of the war. The filmmaker's uncle, Minoru Yasui, challenged the constitutionality of the evacuation of Japanese-Americans on the West Coast. He was the plaintiff in an unsuccessful case brought to the U.S. Supreme Court in 1944. Following the war, he remained an active voice for Japanese-American redress (Minoru Yasui is featured in UNFINISHED BUSINESS).

What began as a filmmaker's search for family roots became a complex story of suppressed history, both personal and collective, told through her own memories and those of her father, aunt, and uncle, as well as home movies and family photos, letters, and news footage. A longer version, entitled A FAMILY GATHERING, which provides additional historical context, was produced for "The American Experience" series and is distributed by PBS Video.

FORBIDDEN CITY, U.S.A.

Arthur Dong 1989

56 min.

DeepFocus Productions

"We had to be much better than the Caucasians, or else we wouldn't get the bookings." This film documents the history and performers of the San Francisco nightclub, Forbidden City, a showplace of Asian-American entertainers in the 1940s. Located on the edge of Chinatown, the club, a landmark of top "Oriental" entertainment during World War II, attracted sailors and soldiers, tourists and other white club hoppers with its exotic razzle dazzle. Although the club advertised its performers as "All-Chinese," some were also Japanese, Korean, and Filipino.

Several former entertainers, now senior citizens, recall their determination to enter show business despite the disapproval of their old-world families and the many doors closed to them in the racist climate of the 1930s and 1940s. They speak of the joy they shared when club proprietor Charlie Low opened Forbidden City in 1938. (The film points out that while this was an excellent opportunity for Asian-American performers, the club did not welcome Asian-American customers.)

Low discusses his efforts to change stereotypes of Asians by creating all-American shows featuring a "Chinese Fred Astaire," a "Chinese Sophie Tucker," and a crooning "Chinese Frank Sinatra." When he added a Chinese bubble dancer a la Sally Rand, his fortune was made. The entertainers in Low's club surprised white Americans, and confused the traditional Chinese community, as well. At Forbidden City, Chinese women showed their legs, men and women danced in Cole Porter revues, and entertainers spoofed Asian and Caucasian stereotypes.

In studio portraits, interviews, performance footage, and clips from a promotional commercial for the club, Low and his entertainers continue to project in age the humor and zest that enabled them as young people to transcend the limitations set by the entertainment industry at the time.

FROM SPIKES TO SPINDLES

Christine Choy 1976

50 min.

Third World Newsreel

A New York Chinatown rally in support of a Chinese-American man unjustly accused of assault and resisting arrest frames this story of Chinese immigration and labor in America. Made in the 1970s, a period of political activism, Choy's film examines the role played by Chinese immigrants in the labor force throughout the nineteenth and twentieth centuries. Chinese immigrant laborers built the railroads and worked in jobs that more established citizens regarded as undesirable, in the garment, restaurant, and laundry businesses.

Concentrating on the New York garment industry, the filmmaker interviews workers, as well as union and city officials, about the industry that has employed many Chinese as well as Jewish, Italian, and Latino immigrants. Unionization of Chinese-American garment workers and the growth of community awareness and vocal protest in the city's other labor markets are highlighted.

HISTORY AND MEMORY

Rea Tajiri 1991

30 min.

Electronic Arts Intermix

Japanese-American videomaker Rea Tajiri had little to go on when she decided to explore her family's wartime experience in internment camps in Arizona and California. There were few photos (cameras were not permitted in the camps) and few openly shared memories of this painful time. Faced only with family silence and fragmented images—real and imagined—Tajiri set out to find the truth of that experience.

Her impressionistic video juxtaposes personal voice-over narration, recollections by family members, and her own memory fragments with family photos, home movies, archival and present-day footage of relocation sites, government propaganda films, and Hollywood films of the period. Densely layering images and memories, the videotape shifts fluidly between past and present. This experimental documentary complements the more traditional family memory films on the World War II Japanese-American internment, such as FAMILY GATHERING and DAYS OF WAITING.

KNOWING HER PLACE

Indu Krishnan 1990

40 min.

Women Make Movies

A candid profile of an Asian-Indian American woman who has struggled to conform to both Indian and American cultures. Suffering from what one might term "cultural schizophrenia," Vasundara Varadhan spent her early childhood in the U.S. and was then sent to live in India. She entered an arranged marriage at the age of 16. The film traces the consequences of this early union and her return to American life as a wife and mother of two sons. Shot over a period of three years, KNOWING HER PLACE allows Vasu Varadhan the space and time to move from a personal sense of cultural confusion and despair to establishing her personal autonomy and professional life. At several points in this process of evolution, Vasu Varadhan frankly discusses her feelings with other women, including her India-based mother and grandmother and videomaker Indu Krishnan, as well as with her husband and adolescent sons in New York.

NISEI SOLDIER: STANDARD BEARER FOR AN EXILED PEOPLE

Loni Ding 1983

30 min.

Vox Productions

This documentary honors the Japanese-American 442nd Regimental Combat Team, the "most decorated unit in U.S. military history." Reminiscences from veterans, archival newsreel footage, photos, radio broadcasts, and newspaper clippings tell the story of the Nisei (second-generation American-born Japanese) men who volunteered to serve their country at a time when they and their families were being held in internment camps. Fifteen-hundred initial recruits joined forces with the 100th Infantry Battalion of Hawaii-based Japanese-Americans to form a segregated Japanese-American fighting unit.

Torn between their loyalties to their incarcerated families and to a country that had betrayed them, these men spearheaded seven major European campaigns. When the war ended, they returned to hometowns where they and their families were rejected and despised. Overcoming the continuing stigma of relocation would be the challenge for the next generation. See THE COLOR OF HONOR, which also deals with Japanese-American military service during World War II. For an account of an African-American military unit during the Civil War, see THE MASSACHUSETTS 54TH COLORED INFANTRY.

SEWING WOMAN

Arthur Dong 1982

14 min.

DeepFocus Productions

Based on the life story of the filmmaker's mother, Zem Ping Dong, and amplified with a series of Chinese-American oral histories, this brief film reveals the dramatic contrasts between a woman's life in China fifty years ago and her experiences as wife, immigrant, working mother, and American citizen. That she survived at all is remarkable, given the fact that her younger sisters were given away or drowned because Chinese families "could not afford to keep daughters."

She recalls how she was groomed for an arranged marriage at 13, and how she and her child remained in China when her husband went to America, not to return until after World War II. In order to join her husband in the United States, she was forced to disown her first son and remarry her husband as a "war bride" (expedited by the War Brides Act of 1945). Haunted by the memory of the child left behind, she nonetheless adapted to America, had more children, and worked in San Francisco garment factories for over thirty years. Her savings and a change in immigration laws enabled her, finally, to bring her first-born son and her Chinese relatives to America.

Highlighted with vintage and contemporary family photos, this monologue traces the changing roles of Old World Chinese and Chinese-American women from the traditional to the modern, and across cultures. It is accompanied by a study guide that provides additional historical detail.

SO FAR FROM INDIA

Mira Nair 1982

49 min.

Filmakers Library

Filmmaker Mira Nair narrates this documentary exploration of the immigrant experience of one extended Asian-Indian family. Focusing on Ashok Sheth, who moves alone to New York in search of financial improvement soon after his marriage, this film details the rationale and ritual of his arranged marriage, his sheltered life in a once-wealthy family, and the painful effect of his leave-taking on his doting older sisters and his pregnant young wife.

The film follows his shy wife, Hansa, who is caught between the expectation of traditions and the Americanization of her husband. The submissive role of women in India and the conflicts that arise when family members are split between two cultures are especially evident in this open-ended documentary. At film's end, after a visit home by Ashok Seth, Hansa and her son remain behind as he returns to New York. Whether or not he will send for his family remains unclear.

TWO LIES

Pam Tom 1990

25 min.

Women Make Movies

A dramatic film that deals with how dominant cultural ideals of physical beauty can lead to the desire to physically alter one's body. Single California mother Doris Chu, a beautiful Chinese-American woman, first appears discreetly hidden in shadow. Her two daughters, preteen Esther and teenaged Mei, are very much in evidence, however. Esther is hard at work building a clay Indian pueblo for a school assignment on "multicultural homes." Their biggest concern is their mother, who has apparently just had an operation to make her eyes look rounder, less Chinese. Mei criticizes her mother for betraying their Chinese heritage and falling victim to the "two eyes, two lies" syndrome.

A family trip to an "Indian pueblo"—which is not, as it turns out, historically authentic—produces a crisis in this culturally confused family. Confrontations between mother and daughter over their own troubled cultural identities and roles lead to a catharsis for the women, but will leave viewers pondering the contradictions of cultures in conflict.

UNFINISHED BUSINESS

Steven Okazaki 1985

60 min.

Mouchette Films

"I'd never been to Japan. I just had a Japanese face." This quote sums up the wartime experience of over 110,000 Japanese-American men, women, and children who had the misfortune to be living on the West Coast in 1942. When Executive Order 9066 forced their incarceration in internment camps, anti-Japanese sentiment was at its highest. This film looks at the issue of internment through the eyes of three men—Fred Korematsu, Gordon Hirabayashi, and Minoru Yasui—who brought legal action to challenge the constitutionality of the internment to the U.S. Supreme Court. As a consequence of their refusal to obey the evacuation order and their challenge to the U.S. government, they were arrested, convicted, and imprisoned. Their stories are told here through first-person accounts, vintage home movies, scenes from a play about Gordon Hirabayashi's life, archival government film footage, and contemporary clips that bring their struggle to vindicate themselves up to the present day. A strong companion piece to FAMILY GATHERING, which profiles Minoru Yasui's family during and after this same period.

WHO KILLED VINCENT CHIN?
Renee Tajima and
Christine Choy 1988
82 min.
Filmakers Library

This provocative documentary, which takes place in economically-troubled Detroit, examines the 1982 killing of Chinese-American Vincent Chin. The film focuses on Ronald Ebans, a one-time foreman at Chrysler Motors who beat 27-year-old Vincent Chin to death following a barroom brawl, and on Chin's mother, who fought tirelessly to have the killing of her son tried as a civil rights issue.

Placing the murder in the context of heightened racial antagonism and economic decline in Detroit, the filmmakers examine the rise of anti-Asian sentiment, due primarily to the success of Japanese import and automobile sales in the United States. In the end, when after five years Ebans walks away a free man, lingering questions remain about the relationship between issues of race and social justice.

ALSO RECOMMENDED:

THE COLOR OF HONOR, Loni Ding 1987, 90 min., CrossCurrent Media

An account of the Japanese-American men who served in military intelligence in the Pacific, as well as those who chose to resist military service on constitutional grounds.

MADE IN CHINA, Lisa Hsia 1986, 28 min., Filmakers Library

A trip to China serves as the backdrop for one young Chinese-American woman's voyage of self-discovery.

THE NEW PURITANS: THE SIKHS OF YUBA CITY, Ritu Sarin and Tenzing Sonam 1985, 27 min., CrossCurrent Media

This documentary traces the process by which the Sikh community in Sacramento, California seeks to combine, and keep separate, traditional and American cultural values.

SLAYING THE DRAGON, Deborah Gee 1987, 58 min., CrossCurrent Media

Using film clips and interviews, this compilation documentary examines stereotyped portrayals of Asians, especially women, in American cinema and television from the 1920s to the present.

YELLOW TALE BLUES: TWO AMERICAN FAMILIES, Christine Choy and Renee Tajima 1990, 28 min., Filmakers Library

The filmmakers follow their own families, one fourth-generation Californian, the other immigrant and working class, juxtaposing their situations with media images of Asians, and revealing the contrast between stereotypes and the realities of lived experience.

Forbidden City, U.S.A., courtesy of DeepFocus Productions

La Ofrenda: The Days of the Dead, courtesy of Direct Cinema Limited

Concrete Experiences

CHICANO FILM AND VIDEO AND AMERICAN HISTORY

Chon A. Noriega

> *This tendency on the part of American scholars to refer*
> *to the United States as North America and to take no cog-*
> *nizance of that section of the continent settled by Spain*
> *more than a hundred years before the founding of Ply-*
> *mouth is not only misleading but historically unfounded.*
> *Carlos E. Castañeda, 1932*

> *In the march of imperialism a people were forgotten, cast*
> *aside as the byproduct of territorial aggrandizement.*
> *George I. Sanchez, 1940*

In the U.S. history curriculum, as educator and writer George I. Sanchez demonstrated, Mexican-Americans have been a "Forgotten People" since the conquest of northern Mexico, now the U.S. Southwest, in 1848. While the Treaty of Guadalupe Hidalgo protected land ownership and granted citizenship to Mexicans north of the new border, these rights fell prey to the rapid economic development of the Southwest. Since at least the 1930s, however, Mexican-Americans have initiated various efforts to amend the historical record and secure civil rights.

But it was not until the 1960s, with the emergence of the Chicano civil rights movement, that U.S. government, business, and educational institutions were compelled to respond to the needs and demands of the Chicano community. With increased access to higher education and mass media, Chicanos were able to develop further the historical reclamation begun by Mexican-American intellectuals such as Castaneda and Sanchez. These histories, however, remain isolated on two accounts—ethnic and regional— on the assumption that Chicanos and the Southwest are somehow not "national" issues. Meanwhile, historiographic categories such as "The Sixties," "Labor and the Left," "The Middle Class," and "Gender and Family" for the most part chronicle the experience of Americans of European descent. The Chicano experience calls into question concepts such as "Westward Expansion." From the perspective of Mexican and Native Americans, it is appropriate to speak also of an "Eastern Encroachment."

Because of the inherent dominant perspective in U.S. historiography, Chicano scholars and filmmakers alike realized the need for self-representation as a prerequisite to a more complex and dynamic national U.S. history. Chicano-produced film and video emerged as a direct component of the Chicano Movement, and continues to draw and build upon these activist origins in diverse formats: documentaries, short dramas, feature films, and experimental media. But in its historical thrust, Chicano video also participates in much older efforts to document cultural practices, resistance, and social injustice that have their origins in the early nineteenth century.

Throughout the twenty-five year struggle for equal access to the mass media, most Chicano producers have been independent or noncommercial, often with distribution of their work limited to public television and local exhibition. In the late 1970s, Chicano (along with other ethnic) filmmakers lobbied for increased support from foundations and government endowments. Since the funding sources emphasized humanities-based projects, Chicano filmmakers were able to produce a number of historical documentaries and dramatic adaptations in collaboration with Chicano historians.

Chicano film and video has always been intended for a dual audience: the Chicano community and the mainstream. Nonetheless, the films produced in the 1960s and 1970s placed more emphasis on the function of historical awareness within the Chicano community. I AM JOAQUIN, for example, presented many

Chicano viewers with their first exposure to Chicano-Mexican history outside direct, familial experiences and memories. Today, I AM JOAQUIN serves as a social document of the late 1960s.

The archival research and videotaped oral histories that inform Chicano documentaries add a new dimension to American history. THE LEMON GROVE INCIDENT, for example, uncovers the first successful desegregation case in the United States. In addition, the videotaped oral histories gathered for the film provide new source material on the Mexican-American experience since the early years of this century. The nine-hour interview with Pedro J. Gonzales for BALLAD OF AN UNSUNG HERO (archived at Stanford University), for example, provides rare information on the development of Spanish-language radio in Los Angeles in the 1930s, as well as on the concurrent "repatriation" or mass deportation of Mexican-Americans.

Given the cultural and linguistic differences that shape the Chicano experience, it is important to understand how Chicano videos process and impart their historical information. Thus, the relationship between the audiovisual text, social history, and ethnic culture is a recurring issue. These videos attempt to re-envision the past, but often choose to do so within the parameters of narrative: drama, performance, and docudrama.

Even conventional documentaries bear the stamp of the role of narrative in Chicano culture. This occurs in two ways. First, videos express alternative forms of history-telling drawn from traditional or popular culture. These include the *corrido* (or Mexican folk ballad) and *teatro* (Chicano theater). Both forms were developed in the mid- to late-nineteenth century in the Southwest and function, on one level, as conveyors of news within Spanish-language, Mexican-origin communities.

In the mid-1960s, Chicano activists revived and expanded these forms as vehicles for historical reclamation that could speak to and on behalf of the Chicano community. In THE BALLAD OF GREGORIO CORTEZ and BALLAD OF AN UNSUNG HERO, historical events are told by way of the *corridos* that first documented those events, and in LOS VENDIDOS and EL CORRIDO: LA CARPA DE LOS RASQUACHIS, the use of improvisational *teatro* collapses the distance between history (events) and story (how those events are told to a particular audience), a distance that does not exist in Spanish, where *historia* denotes both meanings.

Second, videos may express cultural attitudes and sensibilities toward history. These include *rasquachismo* (an underdog sensibility) in the video work of El Teatro Campesino and experimental media artists; and *mestizaje* (cultural mixture) in most Chicano videos. BORDER BRUJO, a video performance by Guillermo Gómez-Peña, incorporates *mestizaje* into its form as well as content in order to convey the fragmented social reality of the U.S.-Mexico border. Several documentaries also construct a "poetic consciousness" about the past, and its relationship to present conditions, actions, and possibilities. LA OFRENDA: THE DAYS OF THE DEAD, for example, examines the relationship between the cultural ritual of "Days of the Dead" in Mexico and its socio-political transformation in the United States. I AM JOAQUIN and YO SOY CHICANO, both made within the context of the Chicano Movement, construct a contemporary Chicano identity based upon a five-hundred year history of *mestizo* resistance in the Americas.

While many Chicano feature films draw upon the conventions of Hollywood, traditional or popular Chicano and Mexican forms also can be found within them. Often, in the use of *teatro* or *corridos*, the three-act structure parallels that of the conventional Hollywood narrative. To take one example, THE BALLAD OF GREGORIO CORTEZ operates simultaneously as both Western and *corrido*, the two dominant narrative forms for histories of the Southwest during the Border Conflict era (1830-1930). The fact that the film is in English and Spanish without subtitles allows it to tell two tales about a single event: the Texas Rangers' pursuit and capture of Gregorio Cortez. For an English-only audience, the film appears to be a conventional Western, with the film shot from the posse's point of view; while for a bilingual, bicultural audience, the *corrido* of the soundtrack identifies Gregorio Cortez as an innocent, defiant folk hero. These two story lines—one visual, the other aural—are brought together in the pivotal translation scene at the end of the film.

These videos raise a central question: How can Chicanos (and other groups) depict history, when historians, journalists, and Hollywood films have either distorted, censored, or repressed the history of the Chicano experience? The answer, more often than not, has been to challenge official histories, with their assumption of an objective past and singular point of view. Rather than match tit-for-tat, these works proffer specific stories of the Chicano experience that complicate the accepted versions of U.S. history.

In the final analysis, the use of multicultural video within the U.S. history curriculum offers more than an act of informational affirmative action. There are, after all, solid historical studies that cover the same issues and periods, and in much greater detail. But as historian Anna Nieto-Gómez explained her personal involvement in the production of the video CHICANA: "When I realized that Chicana history was so alien to my students, I developed a visual media to make her story a concrete experience." It is in that "concrete experience" that video can raise important issues of culture, perspective, and difference in the making of U.S. history. Without that all-too-human dimension, as the filmmakers are well aware, Chicanos will remain a "Forgotten People."

FURTHER READING:

Chicano Aesthetics: Rasquachismo. Phoenix: MARS [Movimiento Artistico del Rio Salado], Inc., 1989. Texts by Tomas Ybarra-Frausto, Shifra M. Goldman and John Aguilar.

García, Mario T. *Mexican Americans: Leadership, Ideology and Identity, 1930-1960.* New Haven: Yale University Press, 1989.

Kanellos, Nicolas. "Folklore in Chicano Theater and Chicano Theater in Folklore." In *The Chicano Experience.* Ed. Stanley A. West and June Macklin. Boulder, CO: Westview Press, 1979.   165-189.

Muñoz, Carlos, Jr. *Youth, Identity, Power: The Chicano Movement.* New York: Verso, 1989.

Noriega, Chon. *Working Bibliography of Critical Writings on Chicanos and Film* (Working Bibliography Series, no. 6). Stanford: Mexican American Collections, Stanford University Libraries, 1990. An updated, annotated version will appear in the *Journal of Popular Film and Television.*

Plena Is Work, Plena Is Song, courtesy of Cinema Guild

Reclaiming Ourselves

PUERTO RICAN INDEPENDENT FILM AND VIDEO

Lillian Jiménez

he "call to self," as feminist author Bell Hooks calls cultural and historical reclamation, provides an opportunity to reconsider the agents and chroniclers of history. People of color, particularly Latinos (Spanish- and Portuguese-speaking people of the Caribbean, Central and Latin America), have been notably absent from historical texts except in subordinate positions. The works discussed in this section may be considered acts of historical reclamation made in defense of the self.

The focus here is on independent film and video work that emerged from empowerment movements in Puerto Rican communities, particularly in New York City, starting in the early 1960s. From the beginning, issues of self-representation were inextricably entwined with issues of self-determination and community control, and independent media became an important organizing tool. These films and videos can be viewed as powerful testaments to a history and culture being retrieved from obscurity.

Stereotypes familiar to generations of Americans obscure the diversity of races, cultures, and world views found within Latino societies. The videos described in this guide, which are markedly different from Hollywood and television depictions of Puerto Ricans, invigorate the conventional forms of documentary and narrative in their intention, style, approach, and content.

Hollywood films perpetuate not only many negative stereotypes about Latinos, but the social relations inherent in those stereotypes, as well. For example, commercial films of the 1950s and 1960s such as WEST SIDE STORY and THE YOUNG SAVAGES featured Puerto Ricans primarily as delinquents or social problems. Many of the independent films and videos listed here actively challenge such stereotyped assumptions by presenting Puerto Rican young people, their families, and their communities at the center of efforts to expose and eradicate destructive economic and political influences in their communities. Unlike conventional Hollywood productions, these works reflect a heightened awareness of the complex socio-political and economic forces that shape people's lives.

Independently-produced films present the experiences of ethnic groups from new perspectives, inverting the traditional power relations found in popular cinema, most notably the actions of white male protagonists propelling the narrative. In contrast, these independent productions privilege the point of view of those whose experiences are being portrayed, avoiding use of "outside" experts or narrators. These subjective and authoritative voices and personal points of view provide a rare window on the many protagonists in the shifting drama of American history.

Susan Zeig and Pedro Rivera's PLENA IS WORK, PLENA IS SONG, for example, is a documentary tribute to Puerto Rican working class culture and its African roots. It shows the important role that *plena*, a musical and literary form, has played as a communicator of social movements, both on the Island and on the mainland. Diego Echeverría's LOS SURES, set in New York City's *barrio*, depicts *Santería*, the syncretism of African and Catholic religions, as a survival and coping strategy. Colonial relationships with both Europe and the United States, commonly experienced by Latino people, are explored in works like José García Torres' THE NATIONALISTS, which is about the activities of the Puerto Rican Nationalist Party in the 1950s. Many of these works bring to light long-hidden histories of resistance to inequities.

Experimenting with narrative techniques is one way filmmakers have challenged the voices which are usually given precedence in mainstream media. José García Torres' THE OXCART is one of many Puerto Rican films of the late 1960s

that mixed narrative and documentary forms as part of the search for a cinematic language that would reaffirm a sense of identity and help reclaim a culture. Many of these films passionately recount migration experiences, poor living conditions, inadequate health care, and unequal educational opportunities, while also celebrating tenacious forms of resistance.

The popular media have long perpetuated the myth that Puerto Ricans have no history. These documentary films, on the contrary—with their gritty vérité style, sense of immediacy, eyewitness testimony, and multiple voices—reveal a dynamic and complex past virtually unknown to most mainland Americans. To illustrate the difference, a teacher might excerpt clips from a Hollywood film such as WEST SIDE STORY and juxtapose them with excerpts from THE OXCART or LOS SURES, encouraging students to examine how their assumptions have been shaped by commercial media—in contrast to the ways Puerto Ricans themselves depict their experience.

In many communities of color around the country, the late 1960s and early 1970s were characterized by struggles for community control of education, health facilities, and housing. EL PUEBLO SE LEVANTA was made by media activists to complement organizing activities in New York's Puerto Rican communities. The film not only assaults our traditional expectations of a seamlessly flowing narrative (it opens with a title punctuated by automatic- weapons fire), it also aptly reminds us that for people of color, picking up the camera was an act of self-defense. In this film, Iris Morales, a member of the Young Lords Party, explains how she blamed her parents for the horrible living conditions in her neighborhood until she realized that larger economic and political forces, not her family, created ghettos. This telling remark reinforces the point that Latinos, like other groups, have absorbed not only the negative stereotypes fostered by mainstream media, but the social assumptions embedded within them.

THE DEVIL IS A CONDITION, by Carlos de Jesús, uses jazz and poetry, two driving expressions of the social power movement of the 1960s and 1970s, to explore the human dimensions of a time when urban renewal programs threatened and ultimately destroyed many of New York City's working class neighborhoods. Powerfully blending jazz with imagery of decaying housing, this film interrogates the policies of urban removal of African Americans and Latinos for the profit of an elite coterie of real estate developers.

Several films provide larger perspectives on the complex and often obscured history of the relationship between Puerto Rico and the United States. MANOS A LA OBRA: THE STORY OF OPERATION BOOTSTRAP by Susan Zeig and Pedro Rivera uses government-sponsored archival films and interviews with U.S. government officials to dissect U.S. development policies in Puerto Rico. It asks who has benefited from this relationship, and what the consequences were. It presents Puerto Rican migration to the mainland as a conscious government strategy to alleviate a population and unemployment crisis in Puerto Rico.

Economic policies tested in Puerto Rico formed the basis for virtually all economic development in the Caribbean. Ana María García's LA OPERACION examines another aspect of economic development policies: population control. The testimony of sterilized Puerto Rican women is juxtaposed with the messages conveyed by U.S.-sponsored promotional films in this chilling indictment of government and corporate collusion in the mass sterilization of Puerto Rican women.

Questions of sovereignty and military force converge in THE BATTLE OF VIEQUES, a documentary exposé of the fight of a group of fishermen against the U.S. Navy for control of their fishing waters. Through interviews with local fishermen and U.S. Navy officials, we learn that the tiny island of Vieques, located off the coast of Puerto Rico, is both a naval target practice range and the launching pad for military interventions by the U.S. in Central and Latin America. This film about a seemingly local dispute is actually an examination of the vestiges of colonialism in the Americas.

Several of the films in this section dramatically depict the consequences of migration, with its contradictory qualities of loss and discovery: the disruption of the family and the constantly adapting culture that has sustained generations through hardships. Using still photographs and interviews with elderly "pioneros" (pioneers), Diego Echeverría's EL LEGADO: A PUERTO RICAN LEGACY presents the human face of the Puerto Rican migration story. These first-person narratives portray a vibrant community that developed networks of "hometown clubs" and civic

organizations, and—in collaboration with other Latino groups—used electoral politics to survive, to fight discrimination, and to assert their democratic rights.

Told primarily from a child's perspective, THE TWO WORLDS OF ANGELITA traces the dissolution of one Puerto Rican family after its migration to New York, and shows how the young daughter of the family is affected. By shifting points of view and story-telling voices in surprising ways, this film challenges conventional narratives and sensitively portrays the diverse reactions and coping strategies developed by each member of the family. This film provides insights into how international economic policies influence domestic labor development and are experienced by individual families.

Luis Soto's THE HOUSE OF RAMON IGLESIA deals with the complex psychological consequences of colonialism within a Puerto Rican family caught between the cultures and values of life in Puerto Rico and on the mainland. It can serve as a trigger film for discussions about the impact of racism on the personal development of people of color.

These videotapes, which suggest the complex history and diverse experiences of Puerto Rican people, belie the once-popular "melting pot" theory of assimilation which claimed that distinctive racial and ethnic identities were destined to blend into an all-encompassing American norm. But disparate cultures and races have refused to melt. On the contrary, race and ethnicity are erupting and percolating in wonderful, exciting, and often painful ways.

FURTHER READING:

"Latino Film and Video Images," *Centro Bulletin,* v.2, no.8 (Spring 1990), provides a good overview of the subject. It includes interviews and essays by scholars, filmmakers, and activists. See "Alternative Media Resources" section.

SELECTED INDEPENDENT VIDEOS
LATINO

BALLAD OF AN UNSUNG HERO

Producer: Paul Espinosa

Director: Isaac Artenstein

1983

28 min.

Cinema Guild

This documentary is about Pedro J. González, a noted Mexican-American singer, songwriter, and political activist whose long life encapsulates the racial and cultural struggles of a century of Mexican-American history. It is structured as a *corrido*—a folk ballad about border conflict—interweaving archival footage and photographs, music, and González' own accounts.

Having served as a telegraph operator for General Pancho Villa during the Mexican Revolution, González emigrated to Los Angeles in 1924. He rose from manual laborer to become a well-known singer and recording star, and began the first Spanish-language radio program in Los Angeles in 1928. González helped foster ethnic pride and cultural continuity in the Mexican-American community. This was especially important during the Depression, when 500,000 to 600,000 Mexicans and Mexican-Americans were repatriated to Mexico on the grounds that they were competing with Anglos for scarce jobs.

Harassed by city officials who feared his political influence in the Mexican-American community, González was convicted on a false charge of rape and was sent to prison for six years. He recounts the story of his incarceration, the racist sentiment that fueled it, his efforts on behalf of penal reform, his wife's lengthy but successful struggle to win his release, and their subsequent deportation. The González family eventually returned to live in California.

González' strength in the face of personal injustice, and his struggles on behalf of justice for Mexican-Americans through his music and broadcasting career, have made him the subject of several *corridos*. He is also the subject of a novel, a detective series, a play, a mural, numerous articles, and Isaac Artenstein's dramatic feature film, BREAK OF DAWN. For a dramatic example of how a *corrido* is adapted to film in order to recall and examine Mexican-American experience through the life of a folk hero, see THE BALLAD OF GREGORIO CORTEZ.

THE BALLAD OF GREGORIO CORTEZ

Producers: Moctesuma Esparza and Michael Hausman

Director: Robert Young 1983

105 min. Spanish and English

Nelson Entertainment

Adapted from the study by Américo Paredes and based on an historical incident and a *corrido* subsequently performed within the Mexican-American community, this dramatic feature chronicles, in song (*corrido*) and layered narrative, the story of a man who was falsely accused of murder. Set in Texas at the turn of the century, the tale unfolds at a time when Anglo culture was being consolidated in the Southwest, escalating racial and economic tensions.

Gregorio Cortez, played in Spanish by Edward James Olmos, is accused by the local Anglo sheriff of stealing a horse. A misunderstanding that arises from poor translating by the sheriff's Anglo aide results in an exchange of gunfire that leaves Cortez' brother and the sheriff fatally wounded. Knowing that he won't receive a fair trial, Cortez flees with a posse of six hundred Texas Rangers in pursuit. After an 11-day, 450-mile chase, Cortez is captured, convicted of murder, and sentenced to fifty years in the Texas Penitentiary.

Originally produced for the PBS "American Playhouse" series, the story was filmed in a cinéma vérité documentary style by noted independent director Robert M. Young, who incorporates sepia tones, hand-held camera work, and natural sound and dialogue. Most of the Spanish language segments are not translated, which underscores the cultural and communication barriers that incited racial conflicts between Anglos and Mexicans during this time. In this multicultural, bilingual context, the limitations of a solely English-language point of view are made dramatically clear. In fact, since no subtitles are used, the privileged viewer is the bilingual one. See BREAK OF DAWN and EL CORRIDO for other adaptations of *corridos*. **CN**

THE BATTLE OF VIEQUES

Zydnia Nazario 1986

40 min.

Cinema Guild

An eye-opening history of U.S. intervention in the Caribbean and its effect on one island culture, its economy, and its people. Vieques is a small island municipality off the coast of Puerto Rico, whose economy was originally based on its productive farm lands and fishing grounds. After several centuries of Spanish control, the island was taken during the Spanish-American War by the U.S. Navy, as a location for military operations. Further military expansion took place during World War II, which resulted in the displacement of thousands of farmers and the destruction of the island ecosystem.

This film documents the Navy's eventual control over 75% of Vieques, utilizing the land and sea for storage and testing of high-tech weaponry, military training, and as a staging point for military operations in the Caribbean. Lifelong residents, who avoided migration to the mainland and to New York City, recall their opposition to naval operations and to those native leaders who cooperated with U.S. government interests. Representatives of the Fishermen's Association detail the destruction of the seacoast and fishing grounds by detonated bombs and naval debris, and criticize the use of their homeland as a base of attack on Central America and the Caribbean countries. See PUERTO RICO: PARADISE INVADED and MANOS A LA OBRA for introductions to the history of U.S. intervention in "the last American colony."

BREAK OF DAWN

Producer: Jude Pauline Eberhard

Director: Isaac Artenstein

1988

100 min. English and Spanish with English subtitles

CineWest Productions/ Platform Releasing

A central tenet of Chicano feature film production has been to counteract Hollywood's fictional Chicano stereotypes with historical dramas. If these films represent a "history lesson," it is a lesson that contrasts a generalized history with specific accounts of conflict, resistance, and cultural syncretism. BREAK OF DAWN, an independent feature film showcased on the "American Playhouse" series, depicts Depression-era Los Angeles, and the simultaneous rise of Spanish-language radio and U.S. government-sponsored mass deportations of both Mexican immigrants and Mexican-Americans.

BREAK OF DAWN is based on Artenstein's documentary about the life of Pedro J. González, BALLAD OF AN UNSUNG HERO. The director's own binational experiences underlie the film's homage to the "golden age" of Mexican and U.S. cinéma. BREAK OF DAWN draws upon the highly stylized song of Mexican cinéma, performed by renowned Mexican actor and singer Oscar Chávez. The film also makes strategic use of American and Mexican B-films of the 1930s, in order to recall the period, but also to borrow effective cost-cutting tricks from the past.

CHICANA

Sylvia Morales 1979
22 min.
Sylvan Productions

CHICANA presents the 500-year history of the Mexicana/ Chicana. In its format, style, and theme, this all-Chicana production recalls I AM JOAQUIN, while it also provides a corrective to the implicit male-oriented nationalism of the earlier film. In a visual pun on the still photographs that both films use, CHICANA opens with brief live action shots of women at work in the home, bringing move- ment—the Chicano Movement—into the domestic sphere. In effect, these brief scenes and the persuasive narration privilege the events of daily life, and mark it as an arena for the affirmation and resistance of other social protests.

CHICANA is an initial step in representing a Chicano identity that acknowledges, rather than glosses over gender, class, and political divisions within the com- munity. **CN**

CHICANO PARK

Producers: Marilyn Mulford
and Mario Barrera
Director: Marilyn Mulford
1989
60 min.
Cinema Guild

This documentary traces the history of the San Diego Chicano community of Logan Heights, or Barrio Logan. This is a story of artists and community organizers who resisted the encroachment of freeways and urban develop- ment which divided their community. In the 1920s, Barrio Logan was the second largest Mexican-American community on the West Coast; but the community was uprooted during the Depression, when large numbers of Mexicans and Mexican-Americans were deported under U.S. government policies intended to protect jobs for Anglos.

In the 1960s, Chicano community activists fought to build a park on a parcel of land under the freeway. Civic and cultural pride came together in an historical vision of the Southwest that traced its origins to the mythical Aztec homeland of Aztlán, located in what is now the U.S.Southwest, and continues through the settle- ment of the barrio in 1900. Community residents, artists, and activists discuss the long process of creating Chicano Park, which was finally opened in 1970 on a freeway un- derpass. The park became the site for community events and expressions from cultural performances to murals.

This is a look at a community which set out to re- claim its cultural roots, land, and heritage. For another documentary about an historical Latino community, see

LIVING IN AMERICA: A HUNDRED YEARS OF YBOR CITY. For a look at broader aspects of the Chicano Movement, see YO SOY CHICANO.

EL CORRIDO: LA CARPA DE LOS RASQUACHIS

Artistic Director:

Luis Valdéz 1976

70 min. English and Spanish

El Teatro Campesino

In EL CORRIDO: LA CARPA DE LOS RASQUACHIS the "tent of the downtrodden" of the subtitle refers, in part, to the canvas-covered truck in which the *corrido* presented in this video is performed. *La carpa* (tent) also refers to the tent-theater tradition of the Southwest, while *los rasquachis* (the downtrodden) refers to the Rasquachi family of the *corrido*. The stage curtain consists of the farmworkers' burlap sacks, while a rope—held in the story by *el Diablo/Patrón*—symbolizes the border that Jesus Pelado Rasquachi, the irreverently named Jesus Poor Tramp, must place around his neck. The turning point occurs when Pelado ties the loose end of the rope around his waist, thus internalizing the border.

The *corrido* of Jesús Pelado Rasquachi is actually a play-within-a-play. It is sung (and, by way of a lapse dissolve, performed) for the benefit of Chicano farmworkers, in the back of a covered truck which is taking them to work as strikebreakers. Thus, the history of Pelado's life becomes a parable designed to educate and politicize the farmworkers and, by extension, the viewers of this video.

Televised as part of the PBS "Visions" series, EL CORRIDO also makes use of vernacular language, creating an "insider's" discourse that is somewhat less polite than what is heard in English. See also LOS VENDIDOS and I AM JOAQUIN for other El Teatro Campesino productions. **CN**

THE DEVIL IS A CONDITION

Carlos de Jesús 1972

25 min.

Carlos Productions

An impressionistic exploration of the housing crisis faced by black and Puerto Rican families in many New York City neighborhoods in the late 1960s. During this period, low-income families began spontaneous protests against poor housing conditions: picketing, withholding rent, and squatting in abandoned buildings slated for renewal. In addition to derelict landlords, tenants faced a parade of rats and roaches, garbage- strewn neighborhoods, no heat or hot water, and the ultimate insult—displacement from their homes to make way for the upscale Lincoln Center cultural center. Using a cinéma vérité style, and mixing jazz and poetry with personal testimony, this film is an early effort at self-representation connected with emerging protests.

DISTANT WATER

Carlos Avila 1990

28 min. English and Spanish with English subtitles

Carlos Avila

The Zoot Suit Riots in Los Angeles in 1943 serve as the backdrop for this bittersweet drama about the impact of segregation on a ten-year-old Mexican-American boy. Previously naive to the racist ways of the Anglo world, Frankie Montoya experiences firsthand the fear felt by male Latinos—the brothers, fathers, and sons of Mexican-Americans fighting in World War II—who were being stripped and beaten by Anglo sailors home on leave.

Frankie and his two young friends must not only run and hide from these "zoot suit brigades," but must also confront their Anglo peers who mock them as "wetbacks" and deride them for being allowed to swim in the community pool only on Wednesdays, after which the pool is cleaned for the week. When Frankie realizes that the so-called system of pool sharing is, in fact, a racist attempt to segregate and demean Mexican-Americans, he and his friends must take a stand.

The film evokes the cinematic styles of the period depicted, examining day-to-day acts of political resistance and cultural affirmation. For other examples of history told from a child's point of view, see also THE LEMON GROVE INCIDENT and THE TWO WORLDS OF ANGELITA.

THE HOUSE OF RAMON IGLESIA

Luis Soto 1986

55 min.

DeSoto Productions

Based on the play by José Rivera, who also wrote the screenplay, this dramatic film was produced for the PBS "American Playhouse" series. After nineteen years of living on Long Island, a Puerto Rican father of three grown sons aims to fulfill his dream of moving back to Puerto Rico. He has worked as a school janitor to support his family, put his eldest son through college, and seen his middle son graduate from high school and join the Marines. Now he, his wife, and younger son Carlos look forward to a life in their homeland. Confusion over house payments which have not been legally documented produces long-distance hassles, as do confrontations with eldest son, Javier, whose career aspirations do not include moving to Puerto Rico. In the stress of events, Javier unleashes a lifetime of bottled-up shame for his Puerto Rican roots, embarrassment over his father's janitorial job, and impatience with his father's inability to keep the family's finances in order.

This drama examines the ramifications of self-hatred, isolation, and generational conflict experienced by minorities within an alien culture, as well as some of the complex consequences of assimilation. See also THE TWO WORLDS OF ANGELITA.

I AM JOAQUIN

Luis Valdéz 1969

20 min.

El Teatro Campesino

In the first decade of Chicano cinéma, filmmakers documented social protests and constructed the first Chicano histories from self-conscious nationalist perspectives. These films reveal a diversity of styles and subject matter, as well as a movement toward cultural narrative forms: teatro actos (sketches), *floricanto* (poetry), *corridos* (ballads), and *testimonio*. I AM JOAQUIN, considered the first Chicano film, makes innovative use of photographs, music, and narration to dramatize Rudolfo "Corky" Gonzales' epic poem of the Chicano experience. The poem and film place the Chicano Movement and the search for Chicano identity within the context of Mexican and Southwest history over five hundred years, from its Mexican and pre-Columbian roots through the Vietnam War. Narrated by Luis Valdéz, with improvised music by Daniel Valdéz. This film provides a prologue to screenings of YO SOY CHICANO, CHICANO PARK, and CHICANA. **CN**

EL LEGADO: A PUERTO RICAN LEGACY

Diego Echeverría 1981

26 min.

Aspira Association, Inc.

EL LEGADO tells the story of the evolution of Puerto Rican culture in New York City, beginning with the migrations that began early in the twentieth century. Combining archival film and contemporary footage with personal interviews with pioneros who arrived in New York before World War II, it reveals the vitality of a Latino neighborhood that created strong community institutions and a vibrant culture in the face of racial discrimination and social inequities. See also MANOS A LA OBRA: THE STORY OF OPERATION BOOTSTRAP, on Puerto Rican immigration to the U.S.

**THE LEMON GROVE
INCIDENT**

Producer: Paul Espinosa

Director: Frank Christopher

1985

58 min.

Cinema Guild

This docudrama is about the events that unfolded in
Lemon Grove, California in the early 1930s, when members of the local school board, with support from the PTA
and Chamber of Commerce, attempted to segregate students of Mexican-American descent in a new and inferior
school. This action came at a time of high unemployment
when large numbers of Mexican-Americans were deported because they were perceived as occupying jobs at
the expense of Anglos.

Dramatic reenactments of the events leading up to
the school board's decision to "Americanize" the Mexican-
American children are intercut with interviews with the
former students, including the now middle-aged Roberto
Alvarez. At the age of twelve, Alvarez was the subject of a
test case brought by parents who boycotted the new
school and risked job loss and deportation to file the
1931 court case, *Roberto Alvarez v. The Lemon Grove School
Board*. The California Superior Court ruled that the
school board could not establish separate schools for
Mexican-Americans, although segregated schools for
Asians, African Americans, and Native Americans remained legal in California. The ruling also helped defeat
the Bliss Bill, which would have legalized the segregation
of Mexican-Americans.

The case marked the first successful legal challenge
to school segregation in the United States, predating the
landmark *Brown v. Board of Education of Topeka, Kansas*
(see THE ROAD TO BROWN) decision by over twenty
years. Producer Espinosa adapted dramatic segments
from the original school board minutes and court case,
providing a re-creation of the case and the period that inspired it.

**LIVING IN AMERICA: A
HUNDRED YEARS OF YBOR
CITY**

Gayla Jamison 1987

53 min.

Filmakers Library

This documentary takes viewers to Ybor City in Tampa,
Florida, a community of Cuban, Spanish, and Italian immigrants who settled in the area before 1900 near the cigar factories that had moved to the United States from
Cuba in search of cheap labor. Highlighted with reminiscences of senior citizens who grew up in the community,
the video reveals that this has always been an enclave of
many cultures. Italians, Cubans, and Spaniards lived side
by side in vigorous neighborhoods that held fast to their

own traditions of food, art, music, dance, and games. Social clubs catered to each nationality, providing medical plans and clinics geared specifically to the needs of their ethnic membership, as well as social events.

Now being rediscovered by artists, folklorists, and developers, Ybor City is experiencing a wave of resettlement. Newcomers can still watch cigar makers, domino players, and Cuban bread bakers in action. This culturally rich community was not free of racism, and black Cubans experienced particularly serious discrimination. But individuals who moved to New York in the mid-1930s to escape Jim Crow laws speak about why they have returned in retirement.

MACHITO: A LATIN JAZZ LEGACY

Carlos Ortiz 1987

58 min.

First Run/Icarus Films

Called the most influential band in the history of Afro-Latin music, the "Afro-Cubans" were directed by band leader Frank "Machito" Grillo, a Cuban maracas player who co-founded the band after his arrival in the United States in 1937. Interweaving the history of Machito's career over fifty years with that of modern Latin jazz from its African-Spanish-European roots in Cuba, this film includes archival music and dance footage filmed since the 1920s in such landmark New York clubs as the Cotton Club, Savoy Ballroom, Palladium, and Village Gate. A septuagenarian here, Machito recalls his early years in Spanish Harlem and the golden era of Latin jazz in the 1940s and 1950s, and is seen delighting his current fans at an outdoor concert in New York. Machito's influence on generations of jazz musicians is explored by such jazz greats as Tito Puente, Dizzy Gillespie, Dexter Gordon, and Ray Barretto. One highlight is the extensive music footage which clearly shows how a man, his colleagues, and his music—a fusion of Cuban and African rhythms—have influenced American music and dance throughout this century.

MANOS A LA OBRA: THE STORY OF OPERATION BOOTSTRAP

Pedro A. Rivera and

Susan Zeig 1983

59 min.

Cinema Guild

Juxtaposing contemporary interviews with archival photos, news footage, and clips from U.S. propaganda films, this film provides an uncompromising yet fair assessment of Puerto Rico's economic and political history under U.S. colonialism since 1898. During the twentieth century, U.S. interests moved Puerto Rico away from its farm-based economy to sugar cane production and to petrochemicals. This destroyed formerly rich agricultural lands and, with them, the island's food base, setting up waves of unemployment and migration.

The key economic development plan, Operation Bootstrap, was initiated in the 1950s as a model for economic development throughout Latin America. The theme of Operation Bootstrap was *manos a la obra*, i.e., "put your hands to work." The main objective was to attract U.S. capital to Puerto Rico by offering generous tax incentives, government subsidies, cheap labor, and cooperative local authorities. Government planners came to identify overpopulation as the principal reason for Puerto Rico's economic problems. Consequently, migration to the U.S. mainland, as well as mass sterilization for women remaining in Puerto Rico, was encouraged. Bootstrap planner Teodoro Moscoso and several technical experts, businessmen, and political leaders discuss the implementation and results of Operation Bootstrap, while cameras document the human impact of unemployment statistics, widespread poverty, and massive migration.

Corporate interests, having made short-term profits, moved on to other Third World countries where labor was cheaper. Puerto Rico never became the promised "Showcase of the Americas." This film might be programmed with LA OPERACION, THE BATTLE OF VIEQUES, and PUERTO RICO: PARADISE INVADED.

LOS MINEROS

Paul Espinosa and

Hector Galán 1991

58 min.

PBS Video

Broadcast as part of the PBS "The American Experience" series, this documentary tells a relatively unknown story in American labor history. The film uses vintage photos, period footage, letters, and interviews with Mexican-Americans and Anglos who grew up and worked in the copper-mining towns of southeast Arizona. Opening with the turn-of-the-century recruitment of Mexican miners to the sister towns of Clifton-Morenci, the program documents fifty years of the lives of immigrant miners and their families. Mexican-Americans were given the dirtiest, most dangerous jobs in the copper mines, paid half the wages paid to Anglos, and were forced to settle in the most undesirable areas of town.

As the copper company grew and prospered during the boom years of the 1910s, Mexican-Americans reaped none of the rewards. Cheated in the company store, subjected to segregated facilities and racial taunts, they attempted to strike for equal wages and better treatment as early as 1903. But despite their large numbers and strong leaders, the mining companies were able to prevail, resulting in the death or imprisonment of many union leaders. Sons of these early miners recall the poor living conditions, segregation, and racism in company towns and how the men suffered injury and death from mine-related diseases or accidents. Although many of them were U.S. citizens, miners also faced deportation under the Depression-era repatriation policy.

During World War II, Mexican-Americans distinguished themselves in battle (winning more medals than any other ethnic group in the war), and were no longer willing to accept an underdog role. In this videotape, several veterans detail their successful post-war efforts to unionize and acquire for miners—after fifty years of struggle—union recognition, equal pay, and benefits.

THE NATIONALISTS

José García Torres 1973

28 min. English and Spanish
with English subtitles
Cinema Guild

Produced for the community-based "Realidades" television series in New York City, this early documentary summarizes the history, principal leaders, and rationale of the revolutionary Puerto Rican Nationalist Party. The events of the 1950s, including the 1954 raid on the U.S. Congress and the contributions of leader Don Pedro Albizu Campos, are presented through newsreels, still photographs, and interviews with relatives and supporters in the United States and Puerto Rico.

LA OFRENDA: THE DAYS OF THE DEAD

Lourdes Portillo and
Susana Muñoz 1989
50 min. English and Spanish
with English subtitles
Direct Cinema Limited

A documentary that examines, through personal accounts and community ceremonies, the history and present-day celebration of El Día de Muertos, the Day of the Dead, in Mexico and in Chicano communities in the U.S. The dead are believed to revisit loved ones at midnight during the first days of November in the culmination of a religious and cultural ritual that is shown to have its roots in Spanish Catholicism and ancient Aztec concepts of life, death, and the afterlife. The evolution of such icons as the skull (symbol of dual existence) is seen in the context of elaborate feast days that include decorating home altars and cemetery tombstones with photos of the deceased, favorite foods, flowers, gifts, candles, and the familiar—often comical—skulls and skeletons. Children as well as the elderly play an integral part in the preparations that enable the dead to "find their way home."

This film explores the relationship between cultural ritual in Mexico and its social and political transformations in the United States. In addition to Mexican-based festivities, members of the Chicano community in San Francisco reflect on the importance of the ritual as a positive connection to their cultural roots. **CN**

LA OPERACION

Ana María García 1982
40 min.
Cinema Guild

By 1974, more than one-third of all Puerto Rican women had been sterilized, and the number continued to grow as a result of a U.S.-sponsored program of population control. The program was presented as part of a strategy designed to reduce population and promote employment in Puerto Rico. Sterilized women, it was argued, would function more productively as part of a reliable work force, unimpeded by the responsibilities of child care.

This film documents in personal as well as political terms how the sterilization policy, which began in the late 1930s, was rooted in U.S. colonial and economic interests. Impoverished women were strongly encouraged to be sterilized, but were given little or no explanation of the procedures involved or the long-term consequences. Many consented, believing that the operation was reversible. Interviews with physicians, film clips of typical sterilization procedures, and commentary from women who underwent the procedure emphasize the social and cultural implications of this policy. Government films extolling the virtues of sterilization are also included. See also MANOS A LA OBRA for a history of Operation Bootstrap.

THE OXCART

José García Torres 1972

20 min. Spanish with English subtitles

Cinema Guild

Selected scenes from "La Carreta" (The Oxcart), a play by Puerto Rican playwright René Marqués, dramatize the dilemmas of Puerto Rican family members preparing to migrate to New York City in search of work. A painful intergenerational family discussion between grandfather, daughter, and grandchildren reveals their sense of loss and dislocation at the prospect of leaving their farm home. The agricultural economy on which they have depended has been destroyed by the growing petrochemical industry. While the grandfather stays behind to face an uncertain future, his family confronts the harsh realities of New York City's barrio. The dramatic portion of this video is followed by a brief documentary overview of the conditions that greeted Puerto Rican families like the one seen in "La Carreta," upon their arrival in New York. THE OXCART provides a good example of the roles of art, performance, and documentary film in representing Puerto Rican history. See also PLENA IS WORK, PLENA IS SONG and THE TWO WORLDS OF ANGELITA.

PLENA IS WORK, PLENA IS SONG

Pedro A. Rivera and

Susan Zeig 1989

30 min. English and Spanish with English subtitles

Cinema Guild

A celebration of *plena*, a form of Puerto Rican working class music that blends the sounds of African and Spanish music with lyrics that speak of political and personal celebration and sorrow. Whether performed on street corners, in bars, or by big bands, in clubs or on the radio *plena* has been a voice of Puerto Rican people. In the 1920s and 1930s, *plena* became the rallying cry of striking workers, and the popularity of the form soon spread. In the 1940s and 1950s, *plena* was played in trendy clubs and moved into mainstream popular music. It was brought to the mainland by Puerto Ricans who settled in New York City's *barrios*. *Pleneros* still sing about broken hearts and marital problems, poor wages and workplace exploitation, courtship and community life—carrying on a tradition of oral history passed down through generations.

A brief historical narration bridges vintage black-and-white film clips of various big band and recording stars, as well as festive performance segments by contemporary street *pleneros* in New York and Puerto Rico. The evolution of the hit record *"Alo, Quien Nama?"* is traced from its inspiration during a textile factory strike. This documentary deals with the importance of music as a form of oral history and social commentary, and as a force for social and political change in Puerto Rican culture. See also BALLAD OF AN UNSUNG HERO, EL CORRIDO, and MACHITO.

EL PUEBLO SE LEVANTA

Newsreel 1971

50 min.

Third World Newsreel

This cinéma vérité film documents how one Puerto Rican community in New York responded to the challenges of racism, poverty, inadequate housing, and job discrimination with political activism in the 1960s. A collaboration between the Newsreel Media Collective—which was dedicated to documenting community struggles—and the Young Lords, this film focuses on the activities of the Young Lords in East Harlem. It follows their efforts to take over a local church as a place to feed, shelter, and educate neighborhood people, especially children and senior citizens. Their efforts to create a "people's church" gain local support, in the face of hostile police action.

There are striking black-and-white images of the Young Lords in action, evoking this period of organized protest. The forceful presence of minority women is also highlighted, within the context of the Young Lords. A preliminary introduction to the political activism in this period, and to the Young Lords, would be helpful, since the film lacks descriptive titles or narration.

PUERTO RICO:
PARADISE INVADED

Affonso Beato 1977

30 min. English and Spanish with English subtitles

Cinema Guild

This film documents the ways in which the development of the petrochemical industry in Puerto Rico adversely affected coffee and sugar production, and virtually destroyed local control of the economy and land resources. The film includes archival footage shot during the Spanish-American War, as well as news footage of a violent workers' strike in the 1930s. Location filming portrays a landscape overtaken by industrial pollution and billboards proclaiming the presence of corporate America. Programming this film with THE BATTLE OF VIEQUES and MANOS A LA OBRA will provide students with several perspectives on the effects of the U.S. presence in

Puerto Rico. See YO SOY CHICANO for a contemporary statement from the Chicano community.

LOS SURES

Diego Echeverría 1984

58 min. English and Spanish with English subtitles

Cinema Guild

One of the poorest New York neighborhoods, *los sures* is home to some 20,000 Latinos, most of them Puerto Rican. This South Williamsburg community, located in a twenty-block area, is a microcosm of many neighborhoods in the United States where residents struggle daily with joblessness, inferior housing, and violence. Residents speak about how they deal with community and personal pressures. In speaking for themselves, they also provide insight into the community of *los sures*.

Five articulate individuals define their world as they experience it. They include a young man without education or job training; a college-educated single mother who works with a local women's organization; a woman who finds solace in spirituality; and a local contractor. Their unsentimental and deeply-felt stories show the ways in which their culture serves as a potent resource: the strong role played by family, church, music, and the neighborhood itself that sustains them.

THE TWO WORLDS OF ANGELITA

Jane Morrison 1982

73 min. English and Spanish with English subtitles

First Run/Icarus Films

As the employment promised by American industrial development in Puerto Rico waned, many Puerto Ricans were left with few economic prospects. This dramatic film highlights the long-term effects of American industrialization on Puerto Rican families. The story is told through the eyes of Angelita, a nine-year-old girl who migrates with her parents to the New York City *barrio*, where family members find economic hardship yet again. Not only have they have lost the sustaining ties of extended family and friends in Puerto Rico, they are encouraged to drop their language and culture in order to get ahead. Angelita's father is an early casualty of assimilation, but she and her mother determine to maintain their cultural identity while accepting some things they cannot immediately change.

An accompanying study guide details the history of Puerto Rican-U.S. relations. See THE HOUSE OF RAMON IGLESIA for a drama about another Puerto Rican family similarly torn between two cultures.

LOS VENDIDOS

Producer: José Luis Ruiz
Director: George Paul 1972
25 min.
El Teatro Campesino

A witty send-up of Chicano stereotypes, from the farmworker to the zoot suiter. The filmed play is framed by an introduction to the work of El Teatro Campesino, with references to both the mythic and historic past. The *acto* (skit) and *corrido* are narrative structures that writer Luis Valdéz adapted to theatre and film in the 1960s and 1970s, as a way to tell the history of Chicano people. The *actos* were agit-prop sketches first performed before striking farmworkers in order to inform and motivate them. In the mid-1970s the *corrido* was introduced as a way to address larger issues of history and yet remain grounded in current political struggles. LOS VENDIDOS satirizes stereotypes perpetuated by U.S. popular culture, suggesting that beneath their exteriors are politicized Chicanos. For studies of racial stereotyping, see also ETHNIC NOTIONS, COLOR ADJUSTMENT, and SLAYING THE DRAGON. Other El Teatro Campesino productions in this list are EL CORRIDO: LA CARPA DE LOS RASQUACHIS and I AM JOAQUIN. **CN**

YO SOY CHICANO

Producer: Jesús S. Treviño
Director: Barry Nye 1972
60 min. English and Spanish
with English subtitles
Cinema Guild

The Chicano experience, beginning with pre-Columbian history and culminating in the Chicano civil rights movement of the 1960s and early 1970s, is the subject of this exploration of Chicano history and identity which interweaves musical sequences, interviews, and historical recreations. Historical subjects include the early history of Texas, the Zoot Suit Riots in Los Angeles during World War II, and the Vietnam War. Music, art, and artifacts work here to express affirmation of Chicano cultural heritage.

The film is divided into ten thematic segments. Four sections present profiles of contemporary political leaders: José Angel Gutiérrez, of La Raza Unida Party, Rudolfo "Corky" Gonzáles, of the Denver Crusade for Justice, Reies Lopez Tijerina, of the Federal Alliance of Land Grants, and Dolores Huerta, of the United Farm Workers. These are intercut with sepia-toned segments on historical characters and events, ending on the then-current Vietnam War. See I AM JOAQUIN and CHICANA for historical overviews related to social issues. **CN**

ALSO RECOMMENDED:

AFTER JOAQUIN: THE CRUSADE FOR JUSTICE, Daniel Salazar 1988, 28 min., KBDI-TV: Front Range Educational Media

This examination of the work of Rudolfo "Corky" Gonzáles, and the twenty-year-old Crusade for Justice organization based in Denver, is highlighted with archival film and interviews.

AFTER THE EARTHQUAKE, Lourdes Portillo 1979, 23 min., Women Make Movies; Third World Newsreel

A young Nicaraguan woman who has emigrated to California shortly before the Sandinista revolution is seen in the process of assimilating to American life, in this dramatic film.

FROM HERE, FROM THIS SIDE, Gloria Ribe 1988, 24 min., Women Make Movies

Using imagery from American advertising and films, Mexican melodramas, and literary texts, this is a view of American culture as seen from the other side of the border.

THE HEART OF LOISAIDA, Bienvenida Matias and Marci Reaven 1979, 30 min., Cinema Guild

In the 1970s, Latino tenants on New York City's Lower East Side joined together to take over and renovate buildings which had been abandoned by their owners. This black-and-white film documents one such group.

The editors acknowledge with thanks the participation of Chon Noriega of the University of New Mexico in writing these annotations.

Running at the Edge

NATIVE AMERICAN FILM AND VIDEO

Elizabeth Weatherford

Independent film and video offers Native Americans an opportunity to tell their history in their own voices. These media productions provide keys to a central reality for Native Americans—that Indians and Eskimos remain invisible in America. For many Americans, traces of native people's presence linger in the towns, waterways, streets, and sports team logos that appropriate their names. Few know about the original inhabitants of the land, how their history was interrupted by invasion and settlement, and where and how they live today. Americans have long been fascinated by the popular images of Indians—in books, paintings, photographs, and films—that have been generated since Europeans' first contact with the people. Thus, the society has many assumptions about Indian and Eskimo life which fit centuries-old stereotypes.

A central issue for Native Americans is the nostalgia that the society has for them as eighteenth- and nineteenth-century people, and the lack of interest in their contemporary cultural and political lives. Some Americans have the strong impression that native people are society's wards and impoverished victims, and know little of Indian and Eskimo accomplishments. Few know any details of the struggles of Native Americans for recognition of legal guarantees that have been violated by officials and neighbors.

Independent film and video productions try to counter the stereotypes and misinformation that perpetuate the invisibility of real Native Americans. They examine little-known histories of tribes throughout the Americas, often focusing on the people's efforts to retain their aboriginal rights. They introduce individuals who tell about how they face the enormous bureaucratic system that establishes policies affecting their lives. They generate images of positive accomplishments in tribal America and show the current renaissance of achievement and autonomy.

American Indians and Eskimo/Inuit today live on reservations, in village and rural communities, and in urban centers. Despite decades of government policies intended to acculturate them to the American mainstream, they retain a strong sense of connection to their people and ancestral lands. Approximately six hundred separate tribes, bands, and nations exist in the United States and Canada. In recent decades the native population has been steadily growing and now numbers approximately two and a half million in the U.S. and Canada. Although distinct in cultural traditions, histories, and environmental settings, the people share a concern for preserving traditional skills and values.

Since the 1970s, Native Americans have been the subjects of more than fifteen hundred independent documentaries, short features, and animated works—some by Native American media makers, some by non-natives. They report the news and identify the people that mainstream media often ignore. In fact, independent works address the enormous information gap about all aspects of native life. In such works as IMAGES OF INDIANS, they also critique the durability of stereotypes and the popular culture's ways of perpetuating them.

Many independent documentaries present members of the community speaking as authorities on their own histories. In HOPI: SONGS OF THE FOURTH WORLD, for instance, traditional elders speak of the tribal past, the impact of missionaries, family life, and the rich symbolic world Hopi inhabit in both daily and tribal life. Their individual voices construct a coherent composite picture. It is important to note, however, that it is a Native American cultural value for individuals to speak only for themselves: a single speaker will rarely presume to generalize about "Indian" experience—or even to speak for the group. The overall effect is to

see Native Americans more personally and less as stereotypes, to see the realities of their lives from their points of view.

Several of these productions grow out of Native Americans' increased activism in the past twenty years on behalf of threatened treaty rights. For many, their lands and waters are a sacred trust, the site of their peoples' spiritual history and practices. An appeal for the restoration of treaty rights becomes an appeal for returning much more than land alone. OUR SACRED LAND not only examines the violation of the Treaty of Fort Laramie; it informs viewers how the Lakota lands in the Black Hills of South Dakota are at the center of deep beliefs and spiritual ways.

Pressure to recognize rights can be exerted outside of courtrooms and political demonstrations. In HAA SHAGOON, a Tlingit leader uses the occasion of a Peace Ceremony to call on the State of Alaska to restore river fishing rights and burial lands to his community. In making his appeal public during the ritual, which is seen in this film, he evokes a powerful image of reconciliation. The resulting film served the Tlingit as an effective tool in their dealings with lawmakers.

Recently, native leaders have developed effective campaigns to reclaim other tangible aspects of their history. BOX OF TREASURES and RETURN OF THE SACRED POLE look at the repatriation of cultural treasures and ritual objects which had been taken from the Kwakiutl of British Columbia and the Omaha of Nebraska, respectively.

Customarily, history focuses on the policies and actions of mainstream leaders, and the absence of knowledge about a people's political history—its leaders and their strategies—may imply that they are outside of historical processes or, worse, that they have no history. Several independent productions focus on native leaders of the past and present, as they have guided tribes facing the pressure of white expansion into native lands. In GERONIMO AND THE APACHE RESISTANCE, for instance, what Hollywood movies have shown as Apache savagery is seen in the context of their relentless pursuit by American military forces, and the changing leadership role played by Geronimo. In CONTRARY WARRIORS, the decision of a twentieth-century Crow leader, Robert Yellowtail, to use practical political strategies on behalf of preserving tribal rights, suggests the complexity of political choices for native communities under pressure from white society.

Viewing a life story permits the examination of how historical processes affect individuals, and casts light on how native people create a synthesis of their own traditions and changing circumstances. ...AND WOMAN WOVE IT IN A BASKET... inventively frames the story of a contemporary Klickitat basket weaver who not only practices a traditional native art, but whose work plays a vital role in the culture and economics of her tribe today. Following one Gros Ventre man, I'D RATHER BE POWWOWING shows how Indians living in cities maintain strong ties to native culture and the reservation communities to which they return for family events and powwows.

Today nearly half of all native people in North America live in cities, rather than on reservations. Drawn by jobs and government initiatives, many find themselves encumbered by bureaucracy and plagued by economic and social problems. Life stories effectively portray the dilemma. FOSTER CHILD is an intimate account of a Metis filmmaker who navigates through the intricacies of the Canadian social welfare system in search of his family. Life stories often reveal the human consequences of government policy. RIVER PEOPLE looks at resister David Sohappy and the erosion for Pacific Northwest tribes of their continued access to the Columbia River. IN THE HEART OF BIG MOUNTAIN shows the effects of government relocation programs on one Navajo family inhabiting the contested Navajo-Hopi joint-use lands in Arizona.

Richer historical perspectives can result when native people present their own versions of events. SONGS IN MINTO LIFE shows how native songs organize and represent historical and personal events. In their most traditional form, songs hold spiritual power that evokes the "first times" in which native culture and history locate their origins.

The use of native forms of communication enhances the survival of a community's culture, language, and views. Control of electronic media radically extends this capacity. STARTING FIRE WITH GUNPOWDER documents the success of Canada's Inuit Broadcasting Corporation, the first native television network, which connects and informs remote Arctic communities with media in their own language.

Works by Native American independents are particularly interesting for their exploration of native ways of history-telling, the forms of which can be strikingly different than the more linear and events-focused approach of most American historical writing. THE PUEBLO PEOPLES: FIRST CONTACT portrays the sixteenth-century Spanish occupation of Zuni lands through a traditional recounting by a Zuni elder, as well as academic commentary by Pueblo Indian scholars. A different way of seeing, through the eyes of a Hopi videomaker, is achieved in RITUAL CLOWNS. Through an experimental montage, this production provides a cautionary statement on interpreting cultural differences.

Independent media about Native Americans provides an opportunity to hear native concerns and understand the long histories of native societies. These productions provide material for teachers to explore intricate historical dynamics that continue to shape American society. They may also be used to introduce students to the concept of historical misrepresentation. The complexity and beauty of traditional Native American culture, depicted in contemporary terms by the visual media, offers students a rich exposure to America's original peoples.

SELECTED INDEPENDENT VIDEOS
NATIVE AMERICAN

...AND WOMAN WOVE IT IN A BASKET...

Bushra Azzouz, Marlene Farnum, and Nettie Kuneki

1989

70 min.

Women Make Movies

"I am an enrolled member of the Yakima Indian Nation. My tribe is Klickitat. Most of the things we do come from legends." With these words, Nettie Kuneki begins her story as basket weaver and daughter of a fishing family. ...AND WOMEN WOVE IT IN A BASKET... is a richly textured account of native life experienced and articulated by a native woman. The film's narrative is built on shifting perspectives: Kuneki's reflections, the reflexive voice of the filmmaker/observer, and the mythic voice of Klickitat legend. As they intersect, they give added depth and meaning to one another.

Today Kuneki is one of the few women who still makes baskets. She came to the practice late in life, with the death of her mother. It was only then that Kuneki began to take seriously her role as a bearer of her tribe's culture. The memories she shares in the film connect her to her parents' and grandparents' generations. The art of basketry, as she reflects on its place in her own experience, makes a fine window onto Klickitat culture, as it was linked to all aspects of the traditional life of this middle Columbia River tribe.

She remembers a time when fishing the river and gathering wild foods were the economic and spiritual mainstays of life. The basket was identified with females' roles in the society, where all subsistence activities were performed in a sacred manner, and women's contribution in gathering foods and processing fish was the complement to men's tasks of hunting and fishing. Exceptional use of many period archival photographs and film footage gives Kuneki's recollections a sense of intimacy.

Several myths are intercut with Kuneki's reflections, including one which tells how the cedar tree first gave basket making to the young female gray squirrel. The story outlines social responsibilities for beginning weavers and accounts for the origin of various designs. This telling in legendary time makes a meaningful counterpoint to the human side of basketry, recounted by Kuneki in historic time.

Kuneki also reflects on how the tide of history and social changes have affected her and her people. She examines the basket's role in today's world, where its value is not in its use, but rather as a cultural artifact symbolizing a link with the people's past. Kuneki is shown with family members digging cedar roots for weaving, and digging edible plants, both time-honored activities that can no longer be taken for granted. Themes of cultural preservation, the role of oral culture, modernization, and history's impact on the individual are brought to life with great imagination and immediacy in this documentary.

For a journalistic examination of the treaty rights of Northwest Indian peoples, see RIVER PEOPLE: BEHIND THE CASE OF DAVID SOHAPPY. **ES**

BOX OF TREASURES

Chuck Olin 1983

29 min.

Documentary Educational

Resources

In 1884, the Canadian government prohibited the Kwakiutl Indians of British Columbia from performing the traditional potlatch ceremony, a lavish feast involving dances and ornate masks and garments. Condemned as a display of heathenism, the potlatch was, in fact, an essential element of tribal identity and the tribal economy. In 1921, when a secret potlatch was held, Kwakiutl artifacts were confiscated by the Royal Canadian Mounted Police and eventually sold or displayed in museums.

This film documents the tribe's reclamation of illegally seized artifacts, which are welcomed home to a specially-built cultural center. The efforts by this community to reclaim its tribal heritage include the recording of elders' oral histories, preserving the native language, and teaching children about their cultural history. Continuing political battles over aboriginal fishing and habitat rights, inadequate schools, and health care are also noted. See also RETURN OF THE SACRED POLE.

BROKEN TREATY AT BATTLE MOUNTAIN

Joel L. Freedman 1974

60 min.

Cinnamon Productions

For American Indians, treaties are living documents which guarantee land ownership and special rights of access to lands and waters. BROKEN TREATY AT BATTLE MOUNTAIN is a stinging indictment, showing how the federal government continues to act in bad faith with Indian nations—in this case, the Western Shoshone of Nevada.

The 1863 Treaty of Ruby Valley, which gave certain rights to the U.S. government, acknowledged the tribe's ownership of twenty-four million acres in Nevada, Utah, and Southwestern California. Some areas of this land were later settled, but most came to be considered federal land, national forest, and public domain lands under the control of the Bureau of Land Management. When, in 1951, the tribe took up its land claims issues with the Indian Claims Commission, they learned that the agency could not grant them legal title to their lands, but could only pay a monetary compensation, thereby extinguishing title.

The conflict of values between Indian and non-Indian society is powerfully demonstrated in the film. Traditional people living in the Battle Mountain Indian colony speak reverently of Mother Earth as a giver of life to Indian people, the source of animals hunted for food, medicinal plants, and pinon nuts, the traditional staple

food. The film vividly contrasts the activities of the traditional people—gathering medicinal plants and preparing
food—with the destruction of the land and animals by
the Bureau of Land Management and white hunters.

The people of Battle Mountain are shown, treaty in
hand, in confrontational meetings with officials of the
Fish and Game Department, the Bureau of Indian Affairs,
and the Bureau of Land Management. Their frustration
with bureaucracy and the government's revisionist interpretation of Indian-white legal history is palpable. Not all
the Western Shoshone are in agreement; some prefer a
cash payment to obtaining legal title, and the lure of a
money settlement is obvious, given the poverty visible in
scenes of the community. To date, the land claims issues
have not been settled. However, since the making of the
film, the people have united in their struggle for the right
to continue to use the land in the accustomed ways for
hunting, food gathering, and other essential traditional
activities. **ES**

**CONTRARY WARRIORS: A
FILM OF THE CROW TRIBE**

Pamela Roberts and Connie
Poten with Beth Ferris 1985
60 min.

Direct Cinema Limited

This film is about the Crow Tribe's century-long struggles
with the U.S. government to retain their culture and reclaim land in southeastern Montana. The title refers to
the Crow warriors who showed contempt for their en-
emies by riding backwards into battle. If they lived, they
were greatly honored. The film's prime focus is on one
such "contrary warrior," tribal leader Robert Yellowtail, a
self-educated lawyer who served as Superintendent of
Indian Affairs under President Franklin D. Roosevelt and
who was in his late nineties when this film was completed. As the history of abuses against the tribe are cata-
logued—from treaty-breaking and the forced assimilation
of Crow children to white culture, to the decimation of
tribal land, coal, and water rights—Robert Yellowtail is
seen to have been at the forefront of the continuing fight
to regain tribal losses.

In CONTRARY WARRIORS, members of Robert
Yellowtail's family reflect on personal struggles of their
own. The important role of women in Yellowtail's life
and their contributions to tribal resilience are also
stressed. Family, culture, and tribal continuity are
strengthened during the annual Crow Fair, which is jux-

taposed here with archival footage of past cultural and political events.

FOSTER CHILD

Gil Cardinal and

Jerry D. Krepakevich 1988

43 min.

National Film Board of Canada

This intimate film traces the search for family and identity by a young Métis filmmaker, Gil Cardinal. A term used in Canada, "Métis" refers to people whose ancestry is a mixture of Indian and non-Indian. Many Métis strongly identify with their native heritage and the native community. As the "foster child" of the film's title, Cardinal's childhood represents the fate of many Métis children, as well as Indian children in both Canada and the United States, who have been placed in non-Indian foster care. Strong opposition to this practice, which disregards children's ethnic and cultural backgrounds, has stimulated legislation to change the situation.

With little assistance from Canadian welfare authorities and largely through his own efforts, Cardinal is able to locate family members. His moments of connection for the first time to a long-lost family are very moving. Cardinal pieces together his mother's story, how she was raised in a mission school and migrated to the city, and learns of his older brother, an accomplished artist who died only the year before. The foster child's search for his origins uncovers not only a specific family, but also reveals the social conditions—dislocation, poverty, and discrimination—which led his mother to give him up. From his odyssey, Cardinal gains new family ties as well as a greater understanding of what it means to be a native person in Canada. **ES**

GERONIMO AND THE APACHE RESISTANCE

Neil Goodwin 1988

58 min.

PBS Video

Focusing on the legendary Apache leader Geronimo, this documentary is about the survival of the Apaches and their bitter conflict with settlers, miners, and others encroaching on their Southwestern territory. The imprisonment of Geronimo and his small band of followers in 1886 marked the closing of the frontier.

The Apache's twenty-year contest with the U.S. military has been mythologized in American popular culture but Geronimo, who has been widely portrayed as a bloodthirsty savage, is described here as a spiritual leader of the Chiricahua Apache tribe. GERONIMO AND THE

APACHE RESISTANCE contrasts Hollywood myths about the Apache with their historical experiences and contemporary lives. The film includes photographs of Geronimo in his many public personae, from warrior to featured performer in Wild West shows.

In 1886, one-quarter of the U.S. Army was in pursuit of Geronimo and his thirty-seven followers. Upon their capture, the group was imprisoned in locations far from their traditional territories and their children were sent to government boarding schools to promote their cultural assimilation. After twenty- seven years, most of them spent at Fort Sill, Oklahoma, the imprisoned Apaches were released. Interviews with descendants of this group provide an Apache perspective on Geronimo's leadership.

HAA SHAGOON

Joseph Kawaky 1983

29 min.

University of California Extension Media Center

This film illustrates how cultural practices of the past can function for the present well-being of a tribe. Specifically, in HAA SHAGOON, the Chilkoot Tlingit of southwest Alaska revive the use of the Peace Ceremony to call attention to injustice and to bring about a resolution to a conflict with the State of Alaska over their aboriginal lands and fishing rights. Elder Austin Hammond was led through a series of visionary dreams to perform the ceremony, and initiated the idea of a film about it to be used as an advocacy tool with state officials.

The film's title is significant. According to Hammond, it refers to a concept of Chilkoot Tlingit self-identity which incorporates all of the tribe's history and lifeways. The elder expands upon Haa Shagoon, especially its links to ancestral lands around the Chilkoot River and subsistence fishing.

At the time of filming, Hammond believed the community to be threatened by actions of the State of Alaska, including the placement of a weir on the Chilkoot River which impeded the salmon spawn, and the disturbance of their ancient cemetery by the building of a road. In addition, the tribe was not allowed to practice subsistence fishing in the river.

The film records the visually breathtaking Peace Ceremony and explains its dances, prayers, and ceremonial clothing. Songs sung by the two Tlingit clans of

Raven and Eagle to commemorate mythic and family history are effectively used as narration for the film. Juxtaposed with scenes of the Tlingit fishing and engaging in other traditional uses of the river, these stories give a moving sense of the people's connection to nature.

As part of the ceremony, four requests are made to the State of Alaska. The film ends with the ceremony uncompleted. Following this public appeal, the state responded to three of the community's four requests. The dispute thus resolved, the Tlingit completed the ceremony the following summer. **ES**

HOPI: SONGS OF THE FOURTH WORLD

Pat Ferrero 1983

58 min.

New Day Films

The intent of this film is to present a complex portrait of the Hopi cultural ideal, the Hopi Way, as it is seen through the eyes of many different community members. The unique history, world view, and cultural practices that distinguish this people from all others is conveyed through well-chosen interviews and beautifully filmed sequences of people taking part in the tasks of everyday life. These elements are interwoven with archival film footage and photographs and paintings of sacred activities.

The film's structure underscores the Hopi understanding of history as a continuum, opening with an account by a Hopi scholar of the tribe's origins in mythic time, followed by an overview of Hopi in historic times. Having lived for a millennium in mesa-top village sites in northeast Arizona, now the Hopi Reservation, the tribe's history and spiritual identity are inseparable from the place where they live.

Corn is an essential feature of Hopi life, pervasive in religious ideas and practice and a staple food, as well. Corn's growing cycle is seen to correspond to the human life cycle with its stages of growth, marriage, family, and inhering male and female roles. In choosing to film women's activities of processing and cooking corn, and the part corn plays in the stages of a woman's life, the filmmaker emphasizes women's key role in Hopi culture.

Interviews with men and women of different ages—artists, farmers, potters, weavers, and others—reinforce the concept of the integration of daily spiritual life with artistic practice. With depth, humor, and irony, their reflections illustrate that the essentials of contemporary Hopi life remain rooted in the customs and values of the past. An exceptional resource handbook is available from New Day Films. See also WINDS OF CHANGE: A MATTER OF CHOICE for an examination of contemporary Hopi life. **ES**

HOPIIT

Victor Masayesva, Jr. 1982

15 min.

Electronic Arts Intermix

This short piece is an early work by an accomplished Hopi videomaker who has continued to live and work in his home village on the Hopi Reservation in Arizona. Produced for the community as part of an educational project, it provides access for outsiders to activities and values that are most significant to the people. Filmed over the course of four seasons, the tape is non-linear in its presentation of moments of life in the villages— children sledding, women weaving baskets and preserving corn, an eagle tied to a housetop, a spider on a circular spiderweb. For a Hopi audience these images are understood at a deeper level. For example, the spider can be seen as Grandmother Spider, an important figure in Hopi mythology; the eagle, which is sacred, is shown being confined in the period before its use for ceremonial purposes. Without commentary in English, the memorable images work on an intuitive level to present viewers with a native perspective on the life of the community. **ES**

I'D RATHER BE POWWOWING

Larry Littlebird 1983

27 min.

Buffalo Bill Historical Center

This is a portrait of a man whose suburban life as a technician for the Xerox Corporation is combined with strong traditional ties to his Native American heritage. Produced by an all-Native American crew, this documentary follows Al Chandler, a member of the Gros Ventre tribe, on his journey to the Rocky Boys Reservation in Montana to take part in a weekend powwow. During the drive, he discusses the values that contributed to his successful transition to city life, as well as the sustaining importance of his continuing participation in traditional rituals. The powwow becomes a metaphor for the cultural traditions which he passes on to his young son in this gathering of family groups who prepare for the dance ceremony and enter the powwow.

IMAGES OF INDIANS

Phil Lucas and

Robert Hagopian 1979

5-part series

30 min. each

Native American Public

Broadcasting Consortium

This series examines Hollywood films as a source of Native American stereotypes that pervade popular culture. Two programs in the series are of particular relevance here.

Part 1, THE GREAT MOVIE MASSACRE, traces the beginnings of media stereotyping of Indians to Western dime novels which appeared in the 1860s and became the inspiration for Western screenplays during Hollywood's early years. Clips from well-known Westerns and historical dramas show the evolution of depictions of Indians as savage heathens or noble children of nature. While Hollywood studios made efforts to authenticate the customs and costumes of other ethnic groups, Native American tribal customs and clothing were freely mixed and misrepresented in a generic "Hollywood Indian" style.

Film stars and directors discuss their work on films that fictionalize American Indians and Sioux writer, Vine Deloria, Jr., contrasts Hollywood myths with facts about Native American history and culture. Numerous clips highlight this segment.

Part 2, HOW HOLLYWOOD WINS THE WEST, discusses the negative self-image experienced by Native American children who see themselves and their families through the distorted lens of Hollywood films which portray American Indians as villains and savages. An alternative set of possibilities for portraying the past is shown in a children's television program which provides a capsule history of U.S. settlement from multiple points of view.

See COLOR ADJUSTMENT for a study of stereotyping of African Americans on television.

IN THE HEART OF BIG MOUNTAIN

Sandra Sunrising Osawa 1988

28 min.

Upstream Productions

Government intervention has pervaded all aspects of tribal life in the United States. Political decisions made in Washington define Indians' legal status, affect their lands, and determine the education of their children, often establishing their destinies for generations. The issues examined in this videotape take place within this context.

The forced relocation in the 1970s of several thousand Navajos and over one hundred Hopi from their homes received considerable public attention. Makah

Indian videomaker Sandra Osawa looks at Navajos of the Big Mountain area of Arizona, located on land shared by the Hopi and the Navajo for hundreds of years.

In 1882, the federal government made the first of a series of shifting designations of tribal ownership of this area. With energy development, the tribes themselves began to have a greater stake in this disputed area. Controversial legislation by Congress in 1974 abruptly resolved the conflict by ordering the removals.

IN THE HEART OF BIG MOUNTAIN gives background and a brief history of the land dispute, but its real subject is the cost to individuals of the government's action. Elder Katherine Smith is a symbol for Navajo resistance. Shown living in a very traditional way, without running water or electricity, she speaks poignantly of her connection to the land where her ancestors are buried, and the importance of Big Mountain as a spiritual center. She seems equally a symbol of great personal courage and of the helplessness and frustration of Native Americans in the face of government involvement in Indian affairs.

Smith's adult sons and daughters also discuss their experiences of relocation and its aftereffects. One of her daughters, Nancy, left Big Mountain to move with her family to Tuba City, Arizona. A good job and a home paid for by the government were strong factors in her decision to leave. In an interview she describes the spiritual anguish the decision has brought. As a translator for new relocatees, she witnesses firsthand the problems brought on by the move. An increased death rate has been recorded; alcoholism and mental problems are common. Isolated from community and family support systems and torn from the land, the people have suffered. The story of the Smith family is an excellent close-up view of this complex situation. **ES**

OUR SACRED LAND

Chris Spotted Eagle 1984

28 min.

Spotted Eagle Productions

The Fort Laramie Treaty of 1868 guaranteed the Lakota Sioux their traditional and sacred lands in the Black Hills of South Dakota. When gold was discovered there, Congress broke the treaty and confiscated the land, opening it to gold miners and homesteaders. This film details the land issue from the point of view of present-day Sioux who have rejected a multi-million dollar government offer to settle their land claim. Tribal leaders and elders document their grievances, the spiritual basis of their land claims, and the relevance of the Indian Religious Freedom Act of 1978, as well as the tribe's ongoing struggle with government and business interests. See also THE SPIRIT OF CRAZY HORSE.

THE PUEBLO PEOPLES: FIRST CONTACT

George Burdeau and Larry Walsh 1990

30 min.

PBS Video

This video about the first encounter between Pueblo Indians of the Southwest and the Spanish marauders who were searching for the Seven Cities of Gold, places the Native American point of view squarely at the center. Prior to first contact, the Pueblo peoples lived in over one hundred pueblos in what is now New Mexico, Colorado, Utah, and Arizona. The first outsider to appear to the Zuni tribe, in May 1539, was a scout—a Moroccan slave—who was part of an expeditionary force making its way north from Mexico, taking Indian slaves and seeking gold. Imprisoned as a spy, he was killed as he attempted to escape. The next contact between the Pueblo people and the Spaniards occurred with the invasion of Coronado, who violated negotiated peace agreements in his brutal search for the wealthy city of Cibola of which he had heard false rumors from earlier expeditions.

The video opens with the Zuni account of the tribal past, which begins in the origins of the tribe before historical time and continues through the telling of Coronado's barbarous incursion—in which villages were burned, slaves were taken, and children and elders were killed. The continuing account of the storyteller is augmented with scholarly commentary, European engravings, tribal art, and poetic video effects which evoke the startling appearance of the conquistadors in the ancient villages and vast landscape of the Pueblo people.

RETURN OF THE SACRED POLE

Michael Farrell 1990

28 min.

Great Plains National

The Omaha tribe of Nebraska, like the Kwakiutl of British Columbia (see BOX OF TREASURES), are working to restore artifacts of cultural and spiritual significance to their rightful homes. One of the tribe's primary religious objects, a sacred pole, had been confiscated in 1888 and placed in the Peabody Museum at Harvard University. Efforts to regain the pole—part of a broad movement among Native American tribes to reclaim religious traditions and artifacts—were led in this case by a direct descendant of Chief Yellow Cloud, the last chief to hold the pole in his trust. This documentary traces the process by which an early anthropologist employed persuasive tactics to take the sacred object to the Peabody for what she regarded as safe-keeping, thereby stripping an already besieged tribe of a central element of tribal identity.

When the sacred pole is returned, members of the tribe gather in a moving ceremony and processional. The 280 Omaha items remaining in the Peabody Museum were returned in September 1990.

RIVER PEOPLE: BEHIND THE CASE OF DAVID SOHAPPY

Michael Conford and

Michele Zaccheo 1990

50 min.

Filmakers Library

In 1982 David Sohappy and his son were arrested for illegally catching and selling 344 salmon out of season. Their arrest was the culmination of a massive undercover effort by state and federal law enforcement agencies. They were each sentenced to five years in prison. RIVER PEOPLE uses an effective structural device which begins by presenting the case, and a view of Sohappy's way of life, much as non-Indian citizens might see them.

"Nostalgically, it would be nice if Indians could fish wherever and whenever they want—David Sohappy's religion, if it is his religion, is a convenient one." These words from the federal prosecutor in the case against Sohappy reveal a racist attitude and ignorance of history. In fact, Sohappy is a religious leader for a group of Indians who still follow the teachings of the Sahaptin Indian prophet, Smoholla. When the Treaty of 1855 was signed, Columbia River tribes gave up nine million acres and were moved to the Yakima Reservation. During this period of upheaval, Smoholla's vision instructed people to continue living along the river in the old way. Smoholla's great-grandnephew, David Sohappy, and others known as "river people" have kept Smoholla's teachings alive. Sohappy has long fought for Indian fishing rights, and his 1968 arrest led to the landmark Boldt decision in federal court which reaffirmed Indian rights to fish.

The film unfolds the events behind the 1982 case, using Sohappy's story to explore the historic conflict over the resources of the Columbia River and the political controversy over fishing rights and religious freedom. This absorbing account is vividly brought to life through archival film and television news footage, as well as in interviews with Indians living along the Columbia River, and participants in the legal case.

In the past fifty years, the Columbia River has become the source for many hydroelectric plants, a repository of factory waste, and the site of the contaminated Hanford Nuclear Reservation. The Columbia's salmon have suffered greatly from such development,
exacerbating the long-standing competition for the harvest. This is an excellent portrayal of a complex of historical and social forces coalescing around one man who became a symbol for all Indians' treaty rights. It raises pertinent questions about this country's legal system and its treatment of groups whose needs and values conflict with the establishment. **ES**

SONGS IN MINTO LIFE

Curt Madison 1985

30 min.

KYUK Video Productions

With the rapid pace of change in Alaska increasingly affecting the Indian communities of the interior of the state, native groups in these areas have begun to use video as a tool to preserve elders' knowledge for native youth, and to inform the Alaskan public about their traditions and perspectives. Generally, this has taken the form of collaboration with public television stations and independent videomakers such as Curt Madison.

SONGS IN MINTO LIFE documents the song tradition of the Tanana Indians living near Minto Flats. Songs have been an integral, even crucial, part of Tanan Indian life. For example, songs used in the hunting which sustained life in this harsh environment are explained by elders as being given by the animals to man. Songs pervaded traditional life: they were part of ritual performance and recorded events in everyday life.

This tape is loosely structured around the four seasons and the subsistence activities that take place in each. One long sequence follows a moose hunt, including the butchering of the animal. This sequence is important because it illustrates the intimate connection between the native people and the animals which provide their sustenance. While narration provides a frame for unfamiliar activities, the heart of the film is interviews with elders, who seem very much at ease with being videotaped, even as they discuss events of personal tragedy and loss, recalled in song.

It is clear from their accounts that these people's history is in part carried by their songs. The Tanana Athabascan language is only now being put in written form. These moments of collective history lived in the experience of the individual and recorded in song are a precious legacy, one that is in doubt as the community faces the future. **ES**

THE SPIRIT OF CRAZY HORSE

Producers: Michel Dubois and Kevin McKiernan

Director: James Locker 1990

58 min.

PBS Video

Originally broadcast as part of the PBS "Frontline" series, this program details the history of the Lakota Sioux tribe and their century-long struggle to regain and protect tribal lands in the Black Hills of South Dakota. Contemporary footage is intercut with archival film and photographs, tracing events from the massacre at Wounded Knee in 1890 to the confrontation between radical activists and the FBI in the early 1970s. This overview provides information about the political, economic, cultural, and spiritual complexities of contemporary Sioux life and the many opinions within the tribe regarding their possible options. There are several examples of the impact of tourism on spiritual locations and the local economy in this depiction of the Lakota Sioux. See also OUR SACRED LAND.

STARTING FIRE WITH GUNPOWDER

David Poisey and William Hansen 1991

59 min.

Tamarack Productions

In contrast to the United States, Canada has had over a decade of support for radio and television broadcasting made by and for its native peoples. The earliest and most extensive broadcast operation is the Inuit Broadcasting Corporation (IBC), which came about in response to the introduction of television in the far North. The Inuit people wanted to counteract the devastating effects of television on the community and lobbied intensely to participate in the production process.

STARTING FIRE WITH GUNPOWDER is a lively history of IBC, narrated by on-camera host Ann Meekitjuk Hanson, a producer/journalist at IBC since its first broadcast. A vivid sense of Inuit life today comes across in the many generous segments of IBC programming included. The four hours of popular weekly television broadcasts include dramas, documentaries, current affairs, and children's programs. A program inspired by Sesame Street features Inuktitut-speaking characters and culture-specific plots. "Super Shamou," modelled on Superman, follows the tradition of the Inuit shaman who possesses powers of transformation and flight. While they are influenced by mainstream television, IBC's programs reinforce native language and convey Inuit values and cultural traditions to the young.

Equally important is IBC's role in addressing contemporary issues. Its coverage of such topics as spousal abuse, substance abuse, and medical care helps to bring about change. For its widespread and remote audiences, IBC's role in reporting news and serving as a forum for political discussion on such issues as the creation of a new Inuit province is vital. STARTING FIRE WITH GUNPOWDER is both a good introduction to life in the Canadian Arctic and an excellent illustration of a people's empowerment through control of the media. See also CLAIMING A VOICE, about media production by a group of Asian-Pacific Americans. **ES**

WINDS OF CHANGE

Carol Cotter,

Executive Producer 1990

2-part series

58 min. each

PBS Video

Important and contested issues of tribal sovereignty, which place tribal allegiances in conflict with larger economic forces, are the subject of this series. The struggle to retain land rights, to resist the encroachment of mining interests, and to sustain traditional cultural values in late-twentieth century America is common to many tribes in the United States. Part 1, A MATTER OF CHOICE, which is narrated by Hattie Kauffman, a CBS correspondent who is half Nez Perce, shows how these issues are being experienced in the Hopi Nation, and shows how many Hopi synthesize elements of both worlds into their lives. Particularly important here are the portraits of various modern Hopi women and the conflicts they have experienced upon leaving or returning to Hopi. This provides a useful supplement to HOPI: SONGS OF THE FOURTH WORLD, which portrays traditional aspects of Hopi culture.

In Part 2, A MATTER OF PROMISES, Pulitzer Prize-winning Kiowa author N. Scott Momaday takes viewers to the Onondaga, Navajo, and Lummi nations and speaks with tribal people about threats to their sovereignty. Among the topics discussed are efforts to ensure cultural continuity such as political activism, encouragement of marriage within the tribe, and education in tribal schools. But adverse U.S. government policies, economic underdevelopment, and the pervasive influence of consumer values have erosive effects that must be continually addressed. Both programs clearly show the process of synthesis and adaptation, even in the face of overwhelming cultural and political factors, that continues to characterize tribal life.

YOU ARE ON INDIAN LAND

George C. Stoney for the
National Film Board of
Canada 1969
37 min.
Museum of Modern Art

Mohawk Indians living on the Akwesasne-St. Regis Reservation, located on both sides of the U.S.-Canadian border, were guaranteed duty-free passage across the international borders between the two countries, according to a 1794 treaty. Cinéma vérité footage documents a tribal protest against violations of that treaty in the late 1960s. Their peaceful efforts to block traffic at the U.S.-Canadian bridge led to open confrontations between the Native Americans and border police, and the arrest of tribal leaders. The event and the circumstances surrounding it were filmed by veteran documentarian George Stoney and a Native American film crew, trained and equipped under the innovative "Challenge for Change" film project initiated by the National Film Board of Canada in 1966. This film won a government hearing of the grievances of the Mohawks, and became part of the process of healing a divided community after the demonstration.

See also WINDS OF CHANGE: A MATTER OF PROMISES about the Mohawk Nation.

ALSO RECOMMENDED:

CLOUDED LAND, Randy Croce 1989, 25 min, Native American Education Services College
This is a present-day and historical account of the profound effects, on both the Ojibwe and Minnesota farmers, of a legal dispute over ownership of White Earth Reservation land.

HONORABLE NATIONS, David Steward and Shana Gazit 1991, 58 min., Filmakers Library
For ninety-nine years, the residents of a small town in Upstate New York have leased their properties from the Seneca tribe. As the lease expires, the Seneca wish to renegotiate terms, bringing the interests of the townspeople and the tribe into conflict.

RIGHT TO BE MOHAWK, George Hornbein, Lorna Rasmussen, and Anne Stanaway 1990, 17 min., New Day Films
Mohawks of the Akwesasne Reservation in New York State speak of the interplay between pressures to assimilate and deeply-held traditions in a vital and adapting society, thereby challenging common stereotypes of contemporary Native America.

RITUAL CLOWNS, Victor Masayesva, Jr. 1988, 18 min., Electronic Arts Intermix
An experimental work, both documentary and poetic, that considers the role of the ritual clown in Hopi Indian culture, as seen from within the community and by observer anthropologists.

The editors acknowledge with thanks the participation of Emelia Seubert of the National Museum of the American Indian, Smithsonian Institution in writing these annotations.

Itam Hakim, Hopiit, courtesy of Electronic Arts Intermix

Crossing Boundaries

USING EXPERIMENTAL VIDEO IN THE
HISTORY CURRICULUM

Deirdre Boyle

S everal years ago *The American Historical Review* devoted an issue to the "possibility of really putting history onto film." Guest editor and historian Robert Rosenstone hailed those filmmakers whose works convey some of the intellectual density traditionally associated with the written word, "films that propose imaginative new ways of dealing with historical material." Resisting traditional genres such as the historical narrative or conventional documentary, these filmmakers have invented new forms of cinema that "render the world as multiple, complex, and indeterminate, rather than as a series of self-enclosed, neat, linear stories." It is just such new, rigorous, hybrid forms of film and video that are considered under the heading "Crossing Boundaries."

The fact that these videos are not familiar in form makes the task of presenting them in a history course more challenging, but it is precisely because they offer such a rich opportunity to shake up expectations and engage students more directly in the consequences of historical processes that they are so valuable. These works can be disturbing, puzzling, and even confrontational; students may feel attacked, bewildered or outraged by what they see and hear. But by channelling your students' frustration and confusion into an exploration of what it has meant to be the Other in white American culture, they will become more aware of how racism, sexism, and ethnocentrism have shaped U.S. history to this day.

When the Kevin Costner film DANCES WITH WOLVES provoked debates about how a Native American filmmaker would have told that story, I suggested to my students that they look at a video by Hopi videomaker Victor Masayesva, Jr. My point was that the response to the conventional Hollywood version of history—where a white male invariably mediates events for the assumed white audience—might not be another romantic saga told now from the viewpoint of an Indian, but rather an entirely different kind of storytelling.

In ITAM HAKIM, HOPIIT (We, Someone, the Hopi People), Victor Masayesva, Jr. presents Ross Macaya, one of the last members of the Bow clan, to tell the Hopi emergence story as well as the Hopi version of the Pueblo Revolt against the Spanish. Masayesva, a consummate visual artist, uses vivid images from the Southwest landscape to invest Ross Macaya's tale with three-dimensional clarity and a sense of immediacy. Significantly, Masayesva leaves the text of Macaya's narrative in Hopi. Although there is a dubbed English version of the video, I do not recommend using it, because it is less effective than watching and listening to the story in the original. Reading a transcript of Macaya's stories after the screening can fill viewers in on the precise details. But first provide your students, who are accustomed to being at the center of their mass-mediated, English-language culture, with the frustrating and illuminating experience of being a cultural Outsider.

In addition to startlingly beautiful natural imagery throughout the tape, Masayesva also uses special video effects to colorize the images of the Spaniards on horseback, evoking the near-hallucinatory experience of first seeing those creatures, half-man half-beast, who suddenly appeared and colonized native peoples. These dream-like images of the conquistadors contrast with the hyper-real imagery illustrating the Hopi myths, reversing Western expectations of what constitutes real and surreal. Without knowing the differentiations between informal, archaic formal, and rhetorical style in the Hopi language, the viewer gradually becomes aware of changes in the speaker's intonations as well as in Masayesva's visual style, grasping the differences between a children's song, a personal memoir, and a clan narrative.

With patience, attention, and a willingness to enter into unfamiliar territory, the student viewer can begin to understand something about the time-space continuum of another culture and appreciate different rhythms and values at odds with those inscribed in mainstream American media.

Chicano performance artist Guillermo Gómez-Peña comes from a different culture and speaks with a different voice, style, and urgency. In Isaac Artenstein's video BORDER BRUJO, Gómez-Peña takes on the personas of various figures— healer, *chollo*, DJ, drunk, tourist, sorcerer, border cop—deftly interchanging masks to expose every stereotype and cultural misconception ascribed to people who live on the border. Wearing Day of the Dead skeleton earrings, a necklace of bananas and chilies, a broad sombrero or a wrestler's mask, Gómez-Peña is alternately mournful, menacing, hypnotic, and rude. "Who the hell invited your ancestors to this country anyway!?" he asks. Rolling his r's he trills "RRRRRRomantic Mexico" as his accent slips from stage Spanish to the flat pronunciation of a middle American asking: "Whatever happened to the sleepy Mexican, the helpful *kimosabe*...Speedy Gonzalez, the Frito Bandito?...Were they deported?!" Whether welcomed as cheap labor or persecuted as illegals, viewed as the exotic Other or reviled as do-nothings, the Chicanos whom Gómez-Peña embodies possess many identities but what they share is a surfeit of anger at the way they have been misrepresented and misunderstood.

Like Gómez-Peña, videomakers Tony Cokes and Donald Trammel use anger as a strategy to explore African-American stereotypes and white fear in FADE TO BLACK. The confrontational nature of work that uses anger to explore racism, sexism, or ethnocentrism makes it risky to use. Audiences may feel attacked, so it is essential that you create a safe space for students first to explore their own reactions and then to go beyond them to understand the profound motivations of producers making such work. Underneath great anger lies considerable pain often caused by generations of ignorance, prejudice, and fear.

Less confrontational in style, though no less effective, is work like Shu Lea Cheang's COLOR SCHEMES, which uses humor—irony, sarcasm, and satire—as its primary strategy. Playing with the notion of the laundry color-wash cycle as a metaphor for racial assimilation, Cheang creates an imaginative structure to introduce a cast of multicultural, multi-racial actors who demonstrate how stereotyping has affected their personal and professional lives. Some of their stories are blatant instances of racism but others are more ironic. When one Native American actor said he had played the roles of both cowboy and Indian, a white actor told him: "So, you're an Indian and a cowboy. Be careful you don't shoot yourself." The washing machine door becomes the frame for these interviews, suggesting the confinement to certain jobs and neighborhoods experienced by many racial groups. Washing itself implies assimilation—the fading or bleeding of color suggesting the loss of individual identity when racial distinctions become blurred. But Cheang's vivid characters defy the process, emerging as colorful and vibrant individuals.

Perhaps most challenging to use is the work of a rigorous theoretician like Vietnamese-born Trinh T. Minh-ha, whose work is highly critical of film conventions as well as prevailing attitudes toward women. In SURNAME VIET GIVEN NAME NAM she addresses her own culture, creating a highly complicated and elegant structure to explore the difficulty women have finding their own voices. The title for the film comes from an anecdote in which an unmarried Vietnamese woman claims her status by saying, effectively, that she is married to her country. What this means, especially to Vietnamese women who live as exiles in the United States, becomes one of the film's subtexts.

To create the sense of dislocation experienced by these Third World women, Trinh has her characters speak halting English when reciting the texts of interviews previously conducted in Vietnam and then has them speak Vietnamese when commenting about their own lives in the United States. That they are playing roles is not readily apparent, but as the viewer grows increasingly discomfited and suspicious of what is going on, the situation gradually becomes clearer. The awkwardness of the women's delivery in English is reinforced, first, by the off-centered placement of the camera, which frequently drifts away from the speaker and, second, by the superimposition of the printed text over their monologues, which is usually out-of-synch with the delivery and often illegible. All of these techniques serve to heighten the impression that the speaker is disadvantaged by circumstances beyond her control, a reality experienced by many immigrants as well as by women as a group. Intercut with archival footage of Vietnam, Trinh's characters speak about a life of oppression that has not changed much from ancient times through colonial administration, war-time deprivation, political repression, and cultural exile.

For students of U.S. history, the experience of watching this film is bound to be irritating or perplexing, evoking frustration that not all the facts are made clear and that they are being deliberately confused by the filmmaker. Like ITAM HAKIM, HOPIIT, this film presents a very different concept of narrative than the reassuring Hollywood film purveys. By engaging in an experience of cultural displacement deliberately orchestrated by a deft filmmaker, the viewer forcibly joins the cultural Outsider on her own terms.

Video artists like Marlon Riggs in TONGUES UNTIED, his brilliant poetic manifesto on being black and gay, and Janice Tanaka in MEMORIES FROM THE DEPARTMENT OF AMNESIA, an elegy for her mother and lost childhood spent in a Japanese internment camp, use poetry, performance, music, fragmentary images, humor, and anger to render the feelings, memories, histories, and social conditions of their diverse cultures accessible and understandable, charged with a meaning and dignity otherwise ignored, repressed or undermined by the American melting pot. The very concept of a homogeneous melting pot is dismantled by such work, most whimsically in COLOR SCHEMES, when the actors sit at a dinner table like the disciples at The Last Supper, consuming a meal of TV dinners with gusto and levity as they triumphantly assert their refusal to be subsumed by mainstream American culture.

Challenging to view and analyze, these videos offer the enterprising history professor an unparalleled opportunity to plunge students into a vicarious experience of cultural Otherness, creating for them new perspectives for examining issues of difference in our ongoing cultural history.

FURTHER READING:

Guillermo Gómez-Peña has written numerous articles about border art. You might wish to read "The Multicultural Paradigm: An Open Letter to the National Arts Community," in *High Performance* (Fall 1989), p.19-27 and "Death on the Border: A Eulogy to Border Art," in *High Performance* (Spring 1991), p.8-9.

Robert A. Rosenstone, "History in Images/History in Words: Reflections on the Possibility of Putting History onto Film," *American Historical Review*, v. 93, no. 5 (December 1988), p.1173-1185, considers the relationship of history and film to the teaching of history.

Trinh T. Minh-ha's book, *Native, Woman, Other,* Indiana University Press, 1989, expands upon many of the ideas and issues presented in SURNAME VIET GIVEN NAME NAM.

Copyright © 1992 Deirdre Boyle

SELECTED INDEPENDENT VIDEOS EXPERIMENTAL

BORDER BRUJO

Isaac Artenstein 1990

52 min. English, Spanish, Spanglish, and Nahuatl

CineWest Productions/ Platform Releasing

Performance artist Guillermo Gómez-Peña is a member of a group of artists whose subject is "border culture." In this satiric video, the border is explored as a zone of conflict between U.S. institutions and values and Mexican/Chicano culture. Seated in front of a colorful altar and wearing assorted headgear, Gómez-Peña presents himself as a shaman, assuming the language and style of fifteen different border personalities in a ritual purification intended to expel the evils that flourish in this contested zone. Expressing rage, desire, mockery, and despair, Gómez-Peña speaks in Spanish, Spanglish, Inglenol, and in Indian dialects in a performance that combines Chicano theatre, border poetry, and Latin American literature in a heady brew.

COLOR SCHEMES

Shu Lea Cheang 1989

28 min.

Women Make Movies; Video Data Bank

"I am a direct descendant of the very first human being. Who else can say that?" Originally presented at the Whitney Museum of American Art as a multi-part video installation, this witty videotape uses a washing machine metaphor—soak, wash, rinse, and spin—to explore the ironies of race and assimilation in the United States. In this lively piece, twelve performers gather in their neighborhood haunts—and, finally, over a stylized "Last Supper"—only to be ultimately drowned out by the din of their own garbled voices and the messages of a racially conflicted society. See also LOS VENDIDOS, for a play on ethnic stereotyping specific to Chicano culture; ETHNIC NOTIONS, a study of black stereotypes; and ALL ORIENTALS LOOK THE SAME, a challenging view of Asian American images. IMAGES OF INDIANS looks at stereotyping of Native Americans.

FADE TO BLACK

Tony Cokes and Donald Trammel 1991

28 min.

The Kitchen; Drift Distribution; Video Data Bank

This is a complex meditation, from the point of view of two African-American men, on how race is represented and socially experienced in American culture. Based on a performance monologue by Donald Trammel which is heard in voice-over, FADE TO BLACK presents three simultaneous visual strands: a chronology of Hollywood film titles from 1903 to 1959 runs along the top of the screen; cropped segments of Hollywood films in which blacks appear fill the middle band; and text drawn from several sources, including Louis Althusser, Malcolm X, and Donald Bogle's book *Toms, Coons, Mulattoes, Mammies and Bucks,* appears at the bottom of the screen and during transitions. Rap and hip-hop music, especially that of Public Enemy and N.W.A., add to the multiplicity of voices and images to create a dense, often confrontational, text.

ITAM HAKIM, HOPIIT (WE, SOMEONE, THE HOPI PEOPLE)

Victor Masayesva, Jr. 1984

58 min. Hopi and English-language versions

Electronic Arts Intermix

In this poetic evocation of the history of the Hopi people, one of the last male members of the storytelling Bow Clan, Ross Macaya, interweaves his own personal history with a version of the Hopi Emergence story and an account of the Pueblo Revolt of 1680. His voice-over conversation with the videomaker, and the structure of the videotape itself—which visually parallels the stories being told—suggest a possible continuation of the Hopi storytelling tradition in new media forms. This video is available in both Hopi and English, which creates two significantly different viewing experiences.

MEMORIES FROM THE DEPARTMENT OF AMNESIA

Janice Tanaka 1989

14 min.

Electronic Arts Intermix

Several Japanese-American filmmakers have explored the legacy of their parents' internment during World War II with sensitivity and historical acuity. Janice Tanaka takes a highly experimental approach in this videotape about her mother's life, from her birth in 1919 to her death in 1988. Utilizing a split screen and incorporating a collage of family photos, titles that mark significant events in her mother's life, and voice-over narratives drawn from lively (and unknowing) grandchildren reminiscing about family, this videotape becomes an elegy to a woman whose life was shaped by forces far beyond her control. Other works that unearth long-buried family experiences are FAMILY GATHERING and HISTORY AND MEMORY.

SURNAME VIET GIVEN NAME NAM

Trinh T. Minh-ha 1989

108 min.

Women Make Movies

The lives of Vietnamese women, seen today and in the past, in Viet Nam and the U.S., are observed and interrogated through documentary footage, interviews, poetry, and performance. In this very personal experimental film women tell of war, exile, traditions, and daily lives, and provide a counter to more familiar official stories. SURNAME VIET GIVEN NAME NAM addresses issues of translation and representation in a highly theoretical work which pushes the boundaries of filmmaking practice and intellectual inquiry.

TONGUES UNTIED

Marlon T. Riggs 1989

55 min.

Frameline

The black, gay male experience in America is the subject of this provocative semi-autobiographical videotape. Utilizing dramatic performances, poetry, rap music, interviews, and reenactments, Riggs describes a search for personal identity in hostile environments. In so doing, TONGUES UNTIED provides an introduction to the history and iconography of the gay black liberation movement, and a meditation on how self-identity and social patterns have been changed over time. Moving through many worlds of gay life, the video explores the languages and relationships that form a social world of shared understanding and self-respect. The video represents a collaboration with black gay artists and organizations.

Alternative Media Resources

A GUIDE

Kimberly Everett

T he works described in this volume are representative of the wealth of independent multicultural media making in the U.S. Unlike Hollywood productions, most of these works do not receive mass public exposure, and the probability of finding them in a neighborhood video rental store is low. What are the best sources of alternative media, and how does one find out about them in the first place?

Although locating them may require slightly unconventional research methods, there are many resources available. The primary sources of independent media are specialized distributors, many of which are not-for-profit organizations. Their video collections include artistic, experimental, and documentary works which examine personal, social, and political issues. Some of these distributors also have a commitment to support the production and promotion, as well as the distribution, of these works.

The Distributors/Sources list (see page 129), provided in conjunction with *Mediating History*'s recommended video titles, is a good starting point for identifying sources. The Association of Independent Video and Filmmakers' *AIVF Guide to Film and Video Distributors* (see page 123), is another excellent resource that lists over 200 distributors.

Most distributors publish catalogs which are updated annually. Typically they include current titles with concise annotations, information about speakers' bureaus, lists of awards, excerpts from reviews, the availability of accompanying study guides, and other pertinent information such as film and videomaker biographies and programming suggestions. Be sure to inquire about current catalogs, press kits, and promotional materials when requesting tapes or price information. Note: developing a good working relationship with distributors can have many built-in rewards. It often ensures attentive service and greater access to information about new and upcoming releases, special discounts, and supplementary materials.

Media selectors in educational institutions often prefer to preview tapes as part of the selection/acquisition process. Distributors' preview policies vary and should be clarified during your initial telephone contact. The three most common practices are:

- No charge for preview videotapes;
- A nominal fee for preview videotapes; some distributors will deduct this fee from the purchase price if the material is purchased within a given time period;
- Shipping and handling costs only are charged to the previewer.

Setting up group evaluation screenings in order to discuss the value and potential uses of the videotape accomplishes two goals: it familiarizes colleagues with the resources available and encourages wider use; and their favorable evaluation can help justify purchase. Sometimes it is possible to request previews for specific dates; more often they will be sent on an as-available basis. However, previews should not be used for in-class presentation or public screenings, since many distributors rely on income from rental fees for such uses.

Independent film and videomakers who handle their own distribution are not always able to provide preview copies due to economic constraints. This may seem awkward to those who are accustomed to working with commercial distributors but independent filmmakers are often eager to accommodate your needs by handling requests personally or pointing you in the right direction.

Distributors are not the only resource for locating alternative media. Festivals, media arts organizations, periodicals, and books can also be good sources of information.

Almost every major city in the U.S. hosts at least one film and/or video festival which showcases work by emerging and established independent artists. Often these festivals are held under the auspices of museums, media arts centers, or other cultural organizations. Festivals range in size, organization, and focus. The variety and quantity of festival programs make them excellent places to view and locate new productions. Festival program guides often provide synopses and background material on featured titles and artists, as well as information about distributors. For a comprehensive listing, consult the *AIVF Guide to International Film and Video Festivals* (see page 123). Selected festivals which feature culturally diverse works include:

ASIAN AMERICAN INTERNATIONAL FILM FESTIVAL and ASIAN AMERICAN INTERNATIONAL VIDEO FESTIVAL
Sponsored by Asian CineVision, these annual festivals showcase works by makers of Asian background.
Asian CineVision, Inc., 32 East Broadway, New York, NY 10002, (212) 925-8685

ATLANTA THIRD WORLD FILM FESTIVAL
Invitational festival sponsored by the Atlanta Bureau of Cultural Affairs featuring films from Third World communities in the U.S., Africa, Asia, Latin America, and the Caribbean.
Atlanta Third World Film Festival, 236 Forsyth Street, Atlanta, GA 30303, (404) 653-7160

BLACK FILMMAKERS HALL OF FAME COMPETITION
Competition devoted to expanding opportunities for black filmmakers who are committed to exploring their history and culture.
Black Filmmakers Hall of Fame, P.O. Box 28055, Oakland, CA 94604, (510) 465-0804

CELEBRATION OF BLACK CINEMA
Since its founding in 1981, the CBC has sponsored five film festivals which have highlighted the work of black filmmakers from the U.S., Africa, Europe and the Caribbean. The organization, incorporated in 1987, has also published articles and books (see *BlackFrames*, page 126).
Celebration of Black Cinema, P.O. Box 181210, Cathedral Station, Boston, MA 02118-1210

MARGARET MEAD FILM FESTIVAL
Originally founded as a forum for presenting anthropological and ethnographic films, this festival held at the American Museum of Natural History features documentaries on a range of subjects.
American Museum of Natural History, Department of Education, Central Park West at 79th Street, New York, NY 10024, (212) 873-1070

NATIONAL LATINO FILM AND VIDEO FESTIVAL

A competitive festival which features work by Latino film and videomakers in the U.S. and Puerto Rico. Sponsored by El Museo del Barrio.

El Museo del Barrio, 1230 Fifth Avenue, New York, NY 10029, (212) 831-7272

NATIVE AMERICAN FILM AND VIDEO FESTIVAL

A non-competitive festival which features new documentaries by and about native peoples of North, Central, and South America and the Arctic. Organized by the Film and Video Center of the National Museum of the American Indian.

National Museum of the American Indian, Smithsonian Institution, Broadway at 155th Street, New York, NY 10032, (212) 283-2420

SAN ANTONIO CINEFESTIVAL

The longest running international film and video exhibition showcasing national and international works by and about Latino and Native American communities. Sponsored by the Guadalupe Cultural Arts Center.

Guadalupe Cultural Arts Center, 1300 Guadalupe Street, San Antonio, TX 78207-5519, (512) 271-3151

MEDIA ARTS CENTERS
AND SERVICE ORGANIZATIONS

State and federal arts and humanities councils, as well as foundations, have provided major funding for alternative media. Independent producers have also received substantial support from media arts organizations at the regional and national levels. The programmatic focus of these groups varies. Their activities and services include conferences, publications, festivals, exhibitions, advocacy, and funding along with production and distribution support. Selected organizations which actively promote the work of independent media makers include:

AMERICAN FILM AND VIDEO ASSOCIATION (AFVA)
A national membership organization serving libraries, universities, schools, museums, and other community organizations. It sponsors the American Film & Video Festival and publishes *Sightlines*, a quarterly journal, and a newsletter, the *AFVA Bulletin*.

AFVA, 920 Barnsdale Road, Suite 152, La Grange Park, IL 60525, (708) 482-4000

ASIAN CINEVISION, INC. (AC)
AC provides production support and media information services. It sponsors the Asian American International Film Festival and the Asian American International Video Festival (see page 121). It publishes the *Asian American Media Reference Guide* (see page 126) and *CineVue*, a quarterly publication.

Asian CineVision, 32 East Broadway, New York, NY 10002, (212) 925-8685

ASSOCIATION OF INDEPENDENT VIDEO AND FILMMAKERS (AIVF)
Established in 1975, AIVF advocates for and supports the production of independent media. Its publications include: *The Independent* (see page 128); the *AIVF Guide to International Film and Video Festivals*, and the *AIVF Guide to Film and Video Distributors*.

AIVF, 625 Broadway, 9th floor, New York, NY 10012, (212)473-3400

THE GUADALUPE CULTURAL ARTS CENTER
An arts center devoted to the development and promotion of Mexican-American arts. The center presents activities designed to foster a greater appreciation of Latino and Native American cultures, sponsors the San Antonio CineFestival (see page 122), and publishes *Tonantzin*.

Guadalupe Cultural Arts Center, 1300 Guadalupe Street, San Antonio, TX 78207-5519, (512) 271-3151

MEDIA ALLIANCE
An organization dedicated to advancing the independent media arts in New York State. Programs and services include advocacy, conferences, workshops and forums, publications, and technical assistance.

Media Alliance, c/o WNET, 356 West 58th Street, New York, NY 10019, (212)560-2919

MEDIA NETWORK

A national organization that supports the production and use of films and videos which examine social, political, and educational issues. Programs and services include information assistance, conferences, publications, and fiscal sponsorship.

Media Network, 39 West 14th Street, Suite 403, New York, NY 10011, (212) 929-2663

NATIONAL ALLIANCE OF MEDIA ARTS CENTERS (NAMAC)

NAMAC is an information and advocacy association whose membership includes community, cultural, and media arts organizations as well as independent media artists. It administers a media arts fund, sponsors conferences, and publishes a directory of member profiles.

NAMAC, 1212 Broadway, Suite 816, Oakland, CA 94612, (510) 451-2717

VISUAL COMMUNICATIONS (VC)

VC was the first arts center founded to support Asian-Pacific American media production. Programs and services include photographic archives, exhibitions, distribution, funding, production support, and co-sponsorship of the Los Angeles Asian Pacific American International Film Festival with the UCLA Film and Television Archive Program. Publisher of *Moving the Image* (see page 126).

Visual Communications, 263 South Los Angeles Street, Suite 307, Los Angeles, CA 90012, (213) 680-4462

In addition, there are five national groups functioning under the auspices of the Corporation for Public Broadcasting (CPB). These groups advocate for and support the production of independently-produced multicultural programs for broadcast on the Public Broadcasting Service (PBS).

NATIONAL ASIAN AMERICAN TELECOMMUNICATIONS ASSOCIATION (NAATA)

NAATA supports film, video, and radio productions by and about Asian-Pacific Americans; publishes *Asian American Network*, an organizational newsletter, and provides media information and distribution services through CrossCurrent Media.

NAATA, 346 Ninth Street, 2nd floor, San Francisco, CA 94103, (415) 863-7428

NATIONAL BLACK PROGRAMMING CONSORTIUM (NBPC)

The NBPC facilitates the development of African-American film and video arts. Programs and services include funding, production support, and media information services. NBPC holds an annual "Prized Pieces" competition and publishes *Take One*, a newsletter.

NBPC, 929 Harrison Ave., Suite 104, Columbus, OH 43215, (614) 299-5355

NATIONAL LATINO COMMUNICATIONS CENTER (NLCC)

The NLCC supports the production of media about Latino culture, arts, and history. Professional training assistance, funding, and distribution services are provided.

NLCC, 4401 Sunset Blvd., Los Angeles, CA 90027, (213) 669-3450

NATIVE AMERICAN PUBLIC BROADCASTING CONSORTIUM (NAPBC)

The NAPBC supports the production and use of programs by and about Native Americans for Native American and other audiences. It provides funding, information, and distribution services.

NAPBC, P.O. Box 83111, Lincoln, NE 68501-6869, (402) 472-3522

PACIFIC ISLANDERS IN COMMUNICATIONS (PIC)

The newest CPB consortium supports the production of original programs by and about Pacific Islanders. PIC will administer a media training and professional mentor program, establish a library of programs for distribution, provide production and funding support, and be a focal point for a Pacific Islanders communications network.

PIC, 733 Bishop Street, #170-92, Honolulu, HI 96813, (808) 536-5050

This selective list of information sources about multicultural media includes some academic journals which review film and video of particular interest to historians. Issues of cultural representation and identity are prominent themes in many of these publications.

BOOKS AND REFERENCE GUIDES

ASIAN AMERICAN MEDIA REFERENCE GUIDE, 2ND EDITION
Gee, Bill J., ed. New York: Asian CineVision, 1990. A catalog listing more than 1,000 annotated Asian American audio-visual programs for rent or sale in the United States.

Asian CineVision, 32 East Broadway, New York, NY 10002, (212) 925-8685

BLACKFRAMES: CRITICAL PERSPECTIVES ON BLACK INDEPENDENT CINEMA
Cham, Mbye B. and Andrade-Watkins, Claire, eds. Cambridge: MIT Press, 1988. Essays which examine various aspects of American, British, and African independent cinema.

MIT Press, 55 Hayward Street, Cambridge, MA 02142, (617) 253-5646

CHICANOS AND FILM: REPRESENTATION, RESISTANCE AND ALTERNATIVES
Noriega, Chon, ed. Minneapolis: University of Minnesota Press, 1992. Essays on Chicano culture, history and issues of representation.

University of Minnesota Press, 2037 University Ave., SE, Minneapolis, MN 55414, (612) 624-2516, (800) 388-3863

IMAGES OF COLOR
Compiled by Media Network in cooperation with the Center for Third World Organizing, 1987. A resource guide to media from and for Asian, Black, Latino and Native American communities.

Media Network, 39 West 14th Street, Suite 403, New York, NY 10011, (212) 929-2663

MOVING THE IMAGE: INDEPENDENT ASIAN PACIFIC AMERICAN MEDIA ARTS
Leong, Russell, ed. A collaborative project of UCLA Asian American Studies Center and Visual Communications, Southern California Asian American Studies Central, Inc., 1991. Distributed through the University of Washington Press. Asian-Pacific media makers discuss the growth, purpose, and impact of independent, alternative media.

University of Washington Press, Box 50096, Seattle, WA 98145-5096, (206) 543-4050, (800)441-4115

NATIVE AMERICANS ON FILM AND TELEVISION
Weatherford, Elizabeth and Seubert, Emelia, eds. New York: Museum of the American Indian, Vol. 1, 1981; Vol. 2, 1988. Catalogs listing approximately 600 film and video productions about native peoples of North, Central, and South America and the Arctic.

National Museum of the American Indian, Smithsonian Institution, Broadway at 155th Street, New York, NY 10032, (212) 283-2420

NEWSPAPERS, NEWSLETTERS, MAGAZINES AND JOURNALS

AFTERIMAGE
A journal of ideas and events related to visual and performing arts, including photography, film and video, and hybrid forms. Published monthly, except July and August, by the Visual Studies Workshop.

Visual Studies Workshop, 31 Prince Street, Rochester, NY 14607-1499, (716) 42-8676

AMERICAN ANTHROPOLOGIST
A quarterly journal published by the American Anthropological Association which features cross-field, theoretical, and review articles as well as book and audio-visual reviews.

American Anthropologist, 1703 New Hampshire Ave. NW, Washington, DC 20009, (202) 232-8800

AMERICAN HISTORICAL REVIEW
Published by the American Historical Association, it appears in February, April, June, October, and December of each year and features critical reviews of current publications and scholarly articles related to all fields of history.

American Historical Review, 400 A Street, SE, Washington, DC 20003-3889, (202) 544-2422

BLACK FILM REVIEW
A quarterly magazine which profiles African-American film and video makers and examines trends in black cinematic art. Published by Sojourner Productions with the Black Film Institute of the University of the District of Columbia.

Black Film Review, 2025 Eye St., NW, Suite 213, Washington, DC 20006, (202) 466-2753

CENTRO BULLETIN
A journal devoted to the study of Puerto Rican history and culture, published by the Center for Puerto Rican Studies, Hunter College. Special issues include: "Latino Film and Video," v. 2, no. 8, and "Latinos in the Media," v. 3, no. 1.

Center for Puerto Rican Studies, Hunter College, 695 Park Ave., New York, NY 10021, (212) 772-5689

CINEASTE
A quarterly magazine which examines issues related to the art and politics of the cinema. It features articles, critical essays, interviews, and profiles of makers, as well as book, film, and video reviews.

Cineaste Publishers, Inc., 200 Park Ave. S., #1320, New York, NY 10003, (212) 982-1241

FILM AND HISTORY
A quarterly publication which features review essays as well as brief reviews of films. It is produced by the Historians Film Committee of the American Historical Association and appears in February, May, September and December.

Film and History, c/o The History Faculty, Humanities Department, New Jersey Institute of Technology, Newark, NJ 07102, (201) 596-3300

THE INDEPENDENT
A magazine published 10 times yearly by the Association of Independent Video and Filmmakers (AIVF), which features articles, interviews, and informational listings covering the scope of the independent media field.

The Independent, AIVF, 625 Broadway, 9th floor, New York, NY 10012, (212) 473-3400

JOURNAL OF AMERICAN HISTORY
A quarterly publication of the Organization of American Historians which features scholarly articles, book reviews and notes, news and comments, and film reviews.

Journal of American History, 112 N. Bryan Street, Bloomington, IN 47408-4141, (812) 855-7311

PIPELINE
A newsletter published by the Independent Media Distributors Alliance, a national network of independent, non-commercial and commercial film and video distributors.

Pipeline, c/o Artbase, P.O. Box 2154, St. Paul, MN 55102, (612) 298-0117

VISUAL ANTHROPOLOGY
A quarterly journal produced in cooperation with the Commission on Visual Anthropology. Published by Harwood Academic Publishers.

Visual Anthropology, Box 786, Cooper Station, New York, NY 10276, (212) 206-8900

Distributors/Sources

Annenberg CPB Project
P.O. Box 2345
South Burlington, VT 05407
800/532-7637

Aspira Association, Inc.
1112 16th St. NW, Suite 340
Washington, DC 20036
202/835-3600

Carlos Avila
8051 Lincoln Blvd.,#5
Los Angeles, CA 90045
310/215-0878

Buffalo Bill Historical Center
Buffalo Bill Museum
P.O. Box 1000
Cody, WY 82414
307/587-4771

California Newsreel
149 Ninth St., Suite 420
San Francisco, CA 94103
415/621-6196

Carlos Productions
Carlos de Jesús
55 West 11th St.
New York, NY 10011
212/691-4930

Chinatown History Museum
New York Chinatown History Project
70 Mulberry St.
New York, NY 10013
212/619-4785

Cinema Guild
1697 Broadway
New York, NY 10019
212/246-5522

CineWest Productions/Platform
Releasing
700 Adella Lane
Coronado, CA 92118
619/437-8764

Cinnamon Productions
225 Lafayette St., Suite 1104
New York, NY 10012
212/431-4899

CrossCurrent Media
National Asian American
Telecommunications Association
346 Ninth St., 2nd fl.
San Francisco, CA 94103
415/552-9550

DeepFocus Productions
22-D Hollywood Avenue
Ho-Ho-Kus, NJ 07423
1-800/343-5540

Desoto Productions
Luis Soto
712 N. Gardner
Hollywood, CA 90046
213/966-2600

Direct Cinema Limited
P.O. Box 69799
Los Angeles, CA 90069
310/396-4774

Documentary Educational Resources
101 Morse St.
Watertown, MA 02172
617/926-0491

Drift Distribution
219 East 2nd St.
New York, NY 10009
212/254-4118

Electronic Arts Intermix ARTS FESTI-
VAL SHOWCASES GALLATIN TAL-
ENT

536 Broadway, 9th fl.
New York, NY 10012
212/966-4605

El Teatro Campesino
705 Fourth St.
P.O. Box 1240
San Juan Bautista, CA 95045
408/623-2444

Filmakers Library
124 East 40th St., Suite 901
New York, NY 10016
212/808-4980

Films for the Humanities & Sciences
P.O. Box 2053
Princeton, NJ 08543-2053
800/257-5126

First Run Features/Icarus Films
153 Waverly Place, 6th fl.
New York, NY 10014
212/727-1711

Frameline
P.O. Box 14792
San Francisco, CA 94114
415/861-5245

Great Plains National
P.O. Box 80669
Lincoln, NE 68501-0669
402/472-2007

KBDI-TV
Front Range Educational Media
2246 Federal Blvd.
Denver, CO 80211
303/458-1200

The Kitchen
512 West 19th St.

New York, NY 10011
212/255-5793

KYUK Video Productions
Pouch 468
Bethel, AK 99559
907/543-3131

Mouchette Films
22-D Hollywood Avenue
Ho-Ho-Kus, NJ 07423
1-800/343-5540
    or
548 Fifth Street
San Francisco, CA 94107
415/495-3934

Museum of Modern Art
Circulating Film & Video Dept.
11 West 53rd St.
New York, NY 10019
212/708-9530

National Film Board of Canada
1251 Avenue of the Americas, 16th fl.
New York, NY 10020-1173
212/586-5131

Native American Education Services
College
1305 East 24th St.
Minneapolis, MN 55404
612/721-1909

Native American Public Broadcasting
Consortium
P.O. Box 83111
1800 North 33rd Street
Lincoln, NE 68501-3111
402/472-3522

Nelson Entertainment
335 North Maple Drive, Suite 350
Beverly Hills, CA 90210
213/285-6000

New Day Films
121 West 27th Street, Suite 902

New York, NY 10001
212/645-8210

PBS Video
1320 Braddock Place
Alexandria, VA 22314-1698
800/424-7963

Scribe Video Center
1342 Cypress Street
Philadelphia, PA 19107
215/735-3785

Sony Video Software
1700 Broadway, 16th fl.
New York, NY 10019
212/757-4990

Spotted Eagle Productions
Chris Spotted Eagle
2524 Hennepin Ave., South
Minneapolis, MN 55405
612/377-4212

Sylvan Productions
12034 Washington Pl.
Los Angeles, CA 90066
310/391-0070

Tamarack Productions
311 Adelaide St., #443
Toronto, Ontario
Canada M5A 3X9
416/363-7441

Third World Newsreel
335 West 38th St., 5th fl.
New York, NY 10018
212/947-9277

University of California
Extension Media Center

2176 Shattuck Ave.
Berkeley, CA 94704
510/642-5578

Upstream Productions
420 First Avenue West
Seattle, WA 98119
206/281-9177

Video Data Bank
37 South Wabash Ave.
Chicago, IL 60603
312/899-5172

Visual Communications
263 South Los Angeles St.,# 307
Los Angeles, CA 90012
213/680-4462

Vox Productions
2335 Jones Street
San Francisco, CA 94133
415/474-5132

William Greaves Productions
230 West 55th Street
New York, NY 10019
212/265-8319

WNYC-TV
1 Centre Street, Rm. 1450
New York, NY 10007
212/669-7726

Women Make Movies
225 Lafayette St., Suite 208
New York, NY 10010
212/925-0606

Alphabetical Title List

Subject Index

CULTURE CLASH

The Ballad of Gregorio Cortez
The Bombing of Osage Avenue
Border Brujo
Distant Water
From Here, From This Side
Knowing Her Place
The Pueblo Peoples: First Contact
So Far from India
Tongues Untied
Two Lies
The Two Worlds of Angelita

DESEGREGATION

Eyes on the Prize: America's Civil Rights
    Years, 1954 to 1965
Eyes on the Prize II: America at the Racial
    Crossroads, 1965 to 1985
The Lemon Grove Incident
The Road to Brown

IMMIGRATION

After the Earthquake
Border Brujo
Carved in Silence
El Corrido: La Carpa de los Rasquachis
From Spikes to Spindles
Knowing Her Place
Living in America: A Hundred Years of Ybor
    City
Los Mineros
The New Puritans: The Sikhs of Yuba City
La Ofrenda: The Days of the Dead
Sewing Woman
So Far from India
Surname Viet Given Name Nam
Yellow Tale Blues: Two American Families

LABOR

Eight-Pound Livelihood
Freedom Bags
From Spikes to Spindles
The Maids
Manos a la Obra: The Story of Operation
    Bootstrap
Miles of Smiles, Years of Struggle
Los Mineros

Plena Is Work, Plena Is Song
Puerto Rico: Paradise Invaded
Sewing Woman
Trouble Behind
Two Dollars and a Dream
Who Killed Vincent Chin?

LEGAL ISSUES

The Ballad of Gregorio Cortez
The Bombing of Osage Avenue
Break of Dawn
Broken Treaty at Battle Mountain
Contrary Warriors: A Film of the Crow Tribe
Eyes on the Prize: America's Civil Rights
    Years, 1954 to 1965
Eyes on the Prize II: America at the Racial
    Crossroads, 1965 to 1985
The Lemon Grove Incident
Our Sacred Land
River People: Behind the Case of David
    Sohappy
The Road to Brown
Who Killed Vincent Chin?
You Are on Indian Land

MIGRATION

Freedom Bags
From These Roots
The House of Ramon Iglesia
I Remember Harlem
    Part 2. The Depression Years: 1930-1940
    Part 3. Toward Freedom: 1940-1963
El Legado: A Puerto Rican Legacy
The Maids
The Oxcart
Plena Is Work, Plena Is Song
To Sleep with Anger
Trouble Behind
The Two Worlds of Angelita

ORAL HISTORY

...And Woman Wove It in a Basket...
Ballad of an Unsung Hero
Box of Treasures
Family Gathering
History and Memory
Itam Hakim, Hopiit

The Color of Honor
El Corrido: La Carpa de los Rasquachis
Days of Waiting
Distant Water
Eight-Pound Livelihood
Ethnic Notions
Eyes on the Prize: America's Civil Rights
  Years, 1954 to 1965
Eyes on the Prize II: America at the Racial
  Crossroads, 1965 to 1985
Fade to Black
Family Gathering
Forbidden City, U.S.A.
The Lemon Grove Incident
The Massachusetts 54th Colored Infantry
Miles of Smiles, Years of Struggle
Los Mineros
Nisei Soldier: Standard Bearer for an Exiled
  People
Puerto Rico: Paradise Invaded
Trouble Behind
Unfinished Business
Los Vendidos
Who Killed Vincent Chin?

RITUAL
Haa Shagoon
Hopi: Songs of the Fourth World
Itam Hakim, Hopiit
La Ofrenda: The Days of the Dead
Ritual Clowns

STEREOTYPES
All Orientals Look the Same
Border Brujo
Claiming a Voice: The Visual
  Communications Story
Color Adjustment
Color Schemes
Ethnic Notions
Fade to Black
Forbidden City, U.S.A.
I Am Joaquin
Images of Indians
      Part 1. The Great Movie Massacre
      Part 2. How Hollywood Wins the
        West

Slaying the Dragon
Two Lies
Los Vendidos
Yellow Tale Blues: Two American Families

U.S. GOVERNMENT POLICY - JAPANESE-AMERICAN INTERNMENT
The Color of Honor
Days of Waiting
Family Gathering
History and Memory
Memories From the Department of Amnesia
Nisei Soldier: Standard Bearer for an Exiled
  People
Unfinished Business

U.S. GOVERNMENT POLICY - LAND AND TREATY RIGHTS
Broken Treaty at Battle Mountain
Clouded Land
Contrary Warriors: A Film of the Crow
  Tribe
Geronimo and the Apache Resistance
Honorable Nations
In the Heart of Big Mountain
Our Sacred Land
River People: Behind the Case of David
  Sohappy
The Spirit of Crazy Horse
Winds of Change
      Part 1. A Matter of Choice
      Part 2. A Matter of Promises
You Are On Indian Land

U.S. GOVERNMENT POLICY - PUERTO RICO
The Battle of Vieques
Manos a la Obra: The Story of Operation
  Bootstrap
The Nationalists
La Operacion
Puerto Rico: Paradise Invaded
The Two Worlds of Angelita

URBAN STUDIES
After Joaquin: The Crusade for Justice
The Bombing of Osage Avenue
Chicano Park

The Devil Is a Condition
Distant Water
From Spikes to Spindles
The Heart of Loisaida
I Remember Harlem
    Part 2. The Depression Years:
      1930-1940
    Part 3. Towards Freedom: 1940-1963
El Legado: A Puerto Rican Legacy
Living in America: A Hundred Years of
  Ybor City
The New Puritans: The Sikhs of Yuba City
El Pueblo Se Levanta
Los Sures
The Two Worlds of Angelita
Who Killed Vincent Chin?

WOMEN'S STUDIES
  After the Earthquake
  ...And Woman Wove It in a Basket...
  Chicana
  Flag
  Freedom Bags
  Gotta Make This Journey: Sweet Honey in
    The Rock
  History and Memory
  Ida B. Wells: A Passion for Justice
  In the Heart of Big Mountain
  Knowing Her Place
  The Maids
  La Operación
  A Place of Rage
  Sewing Woman
  Slaying the Dragon
  Surname Viet Given Name Nam
  Two Dollars and a Dream
  Two Lies

Chronological Index

Itam Hakim, Hopiit
Knowing Her Place
El Legado: A Puerto Rican Legacy
Made in China
The New Puritans: The Sikhs of Yuba City
La Ofrenda: The Days of the Dead
Right to Be Mohawk
Ritual Clowns
Slaying the Dragon
So Far from India
Songs in Minto Life
Los Sures
Surname Viet Given Name Nam
To Sleep with Anger
Tongues Untied
Two Lies
The Two Worlds of Angelita
Los Vendidos
Who Killed Vincent Chin?
Winds of Change
    Part 1. A Matter of Choice
    Part 2. A Matter of Promises
Yellow Tale Blues: Two American Families

PAST TO PRESENT
...And Woman Wove It in a Basket...
Ballad of an Unsung Hero
The Battle of Vieques
Box of Treasures
Break of Dawn
Broken Treaty at Battle Mountain

Chicano Park
Contrary Warriors: A Film of the Crow Tribe
Didn't We Ramble On
Ethnic Notions
Fade to Black
From Spikes to Spindles
Haa Shagoon
Hopi: Songs of the Fourth World
Images of Indians
    Part 1. The Great Movie Massacre
    Part 2. How Hollywood Wins the West
In the Heart of Big Mountain
The Legacy of Arturo Alfonso Schomburg
Living in America: A Hundred Years of Ybor
    City
Machito: A Latin Jazz Legacy
The Maids
Manos a la Obra: The Story of Operation
    Bootstrap
Memories from the Department of Amnesia
Our Sacred Land
The Oxcart
Plena is Work, Plena is Song
Puerto Rico: Paradise Invaded
Return of the Sacred Pole
River People: Behind the Case of David
    Sohappy
Sewing Woman
The Spirit of Crazy Horse
Starting Fire with Gunpowder
Uncommon Images: James Van DerZee

Contributing Authors

BARBARA ABRASH is a teacher, administrator, and independent producer whose work focuses on the relationship between independent media and social history. She teaches in the graduate program in Public History at New York University.

PATRICIA AUFDERHEIDE is an assistant professor in the School of Communication at The American University and a senior editor of *In These Times* newspaper.

DEIRDRE BOYLE is a writer, media programmer, and teacher. She is the author of *Video Classics: A Guide to Video Art and Documentary Tapes* (Oryx) and is currently working on a history of alternative video, *Guerilla Television Revisited* (Oxford University Press). She teaches in the graduate Media Studies Program at The New School for Social Research in New York City.

DARYL CHIN is an independent artist, writer, and curator in New York City. He co-founded the Asian-American International Film Festival in 1978, and the Asian-American International Video Festival in 1983.

CHERYL CHISHOLM is a filmmaker, programmer, and educator who has served as Director of the Atlanta Third World Film and Video Festival since 1984. She travels around the country conducting visual literacy workshops.

CATHERINE EGAN directs the Avery Fisher Center for Music and Media at New York University. Her interest in building media collections and working with faculty to use video in more innovative and effective ways has involved her as a programmer, writer, and workshop presenter.

KIMBERLY EVERETT is active in the production, marketing, and distribution of independent and alternative media. She is currently producing a series of oral history videotapes which examine the evolution of the Harlem community through the lives of visionary individuals.

Lᴜʟɪᴀɴ Jɪᴍᴇ́ɴᴇᴢ has been involved in the production, funding, exhibition, and critical interpretation of independent media in the United States. She is the founder and former director of the National Latino Film and Video Festival of El Museo del Barrio in New York City.

Cʜᴏɴ Nᴏʀɪᴇɢᴀ is Assistant Professor of American Studies at the University of New Mexico. He is editor of *Chicanos and Film: Essays on Chicano Representation and Resistance* (1992), and has published articles in *Cinema Journal, Social Research,* and *Aztlan: A Journal of Chicano Studies.* He has also curated numerous Chicano-Latino film and video series in the U.S. and Spain.

Lᴏᴜɪsᴇ Sᴘᴀɪɴ is an assistant professor at LaGuardia Community College of the City University of New York and Director of Media Services, a library-based audio-visual support center. She is also Chair of the METRO Film Cooperative, Vice-Chair of the CECT/CUNY Instructional Media Consortium, President of the Board of Dance Films Association, and Treasurer of the NY Film/Video Council.

Eʟɪᴢᴀʙᴇᴛʜ Wᴇᴀᴛʜᴇʀғᴏʀᴅ is Department Head of the Film and Video Center of the National Museum of the American Indian, Smithsonian Institution. Since 1979, she has presented the Native American Film and Video Festival in New York City. She teaches in the Program in Ethnographic Film and Video at New York University.

Printed in the United States
By Bookmasters